WI

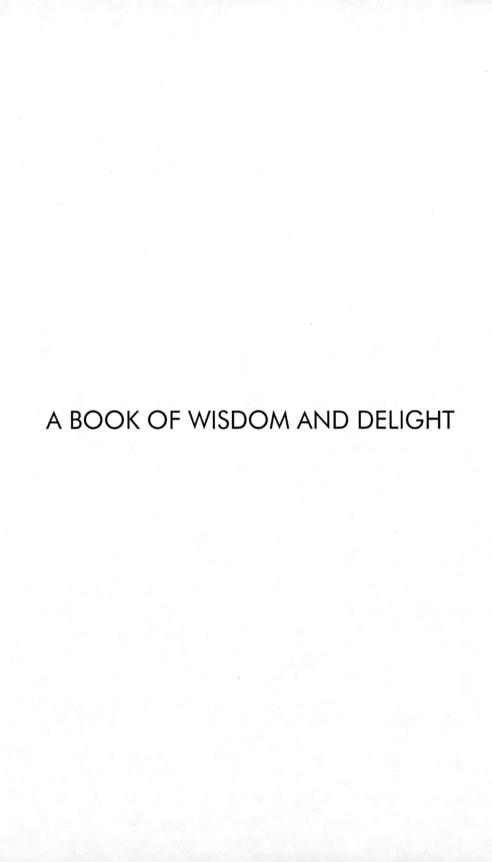

A BOOK OF WISDOM AND DELIGHT

A Book of
Wisdom and Delight

How to Fall in Love with Life

BY JAMES NICHOLAS
Nobel Peace Prize Nominee

iUniverse, Inc.
New York   Bloomington

A Book Of Wisdom And Delight
How to Fall in Love with Life

Yoga images courtesy of Michelle Landry, Digital Dragon Designery, Victoria B.C.
The Scream is courtesy of www.angelo.edu.
Photographs of Saturn, sunflowers, the Pyramids and the
Taj Mahal, courtesy of www.istockphoto.com

iUniverse books may be ordered through booksellers or by contacting:

iUniverse
1663 Liberty Drive
Bloomington, IN 47403
www.iuniverse.com
1-800-Authors (1-800-288-4677)

ISBN: 978-0-595-47537-7 (pbk)
ISBN: 978-0-595-71377-6 (cloth)
ISBN: 978-9-595-91806-5 (ebk)

Printed in the United States of America

Dedication

To my beloved children, Jevone, Tyrone, Dhushyanthi, and Ritesh.

To every person who reads this book and who wants to be wise and happy, I wish that, as you become more aware of your immense potential, you may acquire fine skills in the art of living, which is a difficult art but the greatest of all arts.

Contents

The author, at right, with former United Nations Secretary-General
Boutros Boutros-Ghali and Nobel Peace Prize Winner Mairead
Maguire.

List of Illustrations

Foreword

This book illustrates wonderfully the power of metaphor; it is, indeed, an exercise in metaphor, and it accomplishes its announced intent. It points us indirectly toward a way of being wise and full of beauty. There are aphorisms on every page, beautifully written, charming, and intelligently explained. Simply by following the words, comprehending the language itself, our soul is clarified, for the words create an experience for the mind to act vicariously.

At first I worried that this gentleness would be untrue and overly sweet, like treacle. And certainly there is sweetness there, but it is bracing too—like treacle that we must lick from a thorn, to adapt one of the aphorisms that James Nicholas has quoted.

Do you learn anything practical from this? Yes. In places the book could have been a "self-improvement" volume, like so many others in the junkiest section of today's popular bookstore. There is nothing wrong with the advice of a self-improvement book, and we can even improve ourselves with many of them. But they are not a treat to read. This one does not belong in that section of the bookstore but rather among the poetry books. The advice it offers is valid enough—information about the effects of various types of vitamins, for example, and tips on time management—but it is unexpected for such a book to impart grace and beauty.

—Metta Spencer, Emeritus Professor of Sociology,
University of Toronto

Acknowledgments

The composition of this book is like the composition of an ensemble. While I wrote the lyrics and the notes, the rich quality of the music would not have been possible without the talented players of the ensemble. Their dedication and constructive criticisms were invaluable. This book has a Hellenic effect, thanks to the imagination of Helen Harker, who brightened every area that she touched. Winston Kinnaird's background as a playwright enabled him to add a literary flavor to the book. James Clarkson's ideas were gently suggestive and very powerful, which embellished the book. My thanks to Victor Shulist, who spent painstaking hours in formatting and stylizing. Sharon Johnson, Maire Gannon, Deborah Kerr, Suzanne Dutrisac and Anne Kneif made noteworthy contributions. Kudos to Michelle Landry for designing the cover. A special thanks to all the critics who have so eloquently offered words of commendation. I am grateful to the Canadian National Institute for the Blind for helping me with the team of volunteers who rendered excellent secretarial service.

My profound gratitude to Mairead Corrigan-Maguire, Nobel Peace Prize winner, for writing a commendation that appears on the cover.

My deep appreciation to Professor Metta Spencer, the erudite sociologist from the University of Toronto, for writing the foreword.

This book is spiced with numerous quotations, most of which have been taken from secondary sources whose titles are listed in the bibliography.

I am beholden to all the writers of the musical lyrics that have been quoted.

Prologue

Life is wonderful, though at times it can be hard. In the heart of existence, there is much sweetness to be enjoyed, even in the midst of suffering.[1] Life is also a gift, and how fortunate we are to be living on this incredibly beautiful planet, to behold the infinite diversity of nature. True, we must cope with humid days and freezing nights, but how marvellous it is to observe flowers blooming, fruits ripening, birds singing, and stars twinkling.

Sometimes nature is harsh and cruel. Earthquakes, hurricanes, and volcanoes sometimes strike us with intense fury, causing havoc and immense suffering. While accepting the reality of natural disasters, we must learn to cope with them and not live in fear. We need to be optimistic, because pessimism is a waste of energy.

Nevertheless, nature has inspired me to write this book. I stand in awe at the beautiful balances that pervade it, such as the blended colors of the rainbow and the symmetrical shapes of flowers. From nature we can learn to be like the oak, standing strong against any tempest, or be flexible like the willow, bending gently before any wind.

This work attempts to truly reflect its title as *A Book of Wisdom and Delight: How to Fall in Love with Life*. You are invited to treat this book like a friendly companion, to make you hopeful when *disappointed* and cheerful when *disheartened*. Embodied within these pages are profound ideas of eminent writers that are expressed in simple terms. By reflecting upon their ideas, we can have a "conversation" with them. The book offers challenging but easy reading. It draws enriching ideas from philosophy, psychology, and literature from the East and the West. The thoughts of modern writers intertwine with those of the classics, along with my own reflections. I have quoted other authors profusely only to better express myself.

The principal aim of this book is to present you with *flashes of wisdom and moments of delight*. These sentiments together serve as a refrain that echoes throughout the book. The golden chain that links all chapters together is the belief that the essence of wisdom lies in both balance and proportion. This golden chain starts in Chapter 1, "Enjoy Inner Peace and Calm," which explains that a good inner life enables us to cope better with irritants of our outer life. Inner contentment comes from reconciling our many conflicting desires. We need to harmonize our tendencies to be selfless and selfish, grateful and ungrateful, loving and unloving.

1

In the second chapter, "Give Yourself a Dazzling Mind," we explore how the mind excels when it displays a fine sense of balance and proportion. We discern that flowers are beautiful because the petals and colors form elegant patterns. A great work of music is enchanting because the notes are arranged in a concord of sweet sounds. By further enriching our appreciation of balance and proportion, our minds can sparkle and shine.

What works for the mind can also work for the heart. Typically, we find rest among those we love and provide a resting place for those who love us. This balance in reciprocal relationships is the gist of Chapter 3, "The Joys of Genuine Intimacy." Impressive evidence reveals that when we are more loving in our relationships, we tend to be more joyous and creative. This state contributes to an overall feeling of personal fulfilment.

At a deeper level, sexual love is like a fire that is extinguished when satisfied. It is, therefore, essential to balance sexual love with tenderness and emotional intimacy.

In the fourth chapter, "Be Ever Young in Spirit," I suggest that we balance the toll of passing years by renewing our youthful spirit. With a sense of adventure, wonder, and idealism, we may imagine being young at any age. This chapter also illustrates ways for us to lead a richer life and, in doing so, erase the scars of earlier times. As the fountain of youth is largely a state of mind, we could perennially remain young at heart.

Having a balanced life is a foundation from which we can achieve success. This is the principal point in Chapter 5, "A Blueprint for Success." We can imitate the balance we find in nature in our daily efforts. Just as every crest in the ocean has an ebb, our daily life has ups and downs. From the peak of success, we may slip into setbacks only to profit from them and rise again. A sense of perspective tells us that to achieve great success, we may have to pay a great price. We may also note that, while attaining success may be difficult, sustaining it could be even more so.

To know how to maximize our energy and minimize its loss is a sign of wisdom. These methods are presented in the sixth and final chapter, "Abundant Energy for Everyday Life." We discuss how the energy flowing into us should exceed the energy flowing out to maintain stability of mind and body. In every moment of life, we have thoughts that either strengthen or weaken us. Fear and anger decrease our energy and may confine our thinking. Love and joy increase our energy and may fuel our creative spirit.

All six chapters convey a common message but in different ways. Each one reveals thoughts to ponder on how we may lead the life we desire and deserve. Together, they are an invitation for you, the reader, to plant a tree of Wisdom and Delight and enjoy its growth all your life.

Chapter 1
Enjoy Inner Peace and Calm

Chapter 1
Enjoy Inner Peace and Calm

Human desire is like a thirst. All our life is mainly a quest of how to quench this thirst. The extent to which we are happy depends on the extent to which we can satisfy it. When fulfilled, our deepest desires will provide us with the greatest joys. Our fleeting desires only give us temporary pleasures.

Numerous though our desires may be, they all converge toward the attainment of a single goal: to enjoy inner peace and calm. This is a special type of happiness that is rich and real, deep and enduring. Attaining inner peace is our ultimate desire, our most cherished end.

To enjoy inner peace and calm, it is vital to make decisions wisely and to adjust to pressures smoothly. We need to walk safely on a saner path and to soften the harshness of life. According to Eric Hoffer[2] (1902–1983), the things we often pursue most passionately are but a substitute for the one thing we really want: inner peace and calm.

In this chapter we shall explore ways of enjoying inner peace and calm, how the soul may abide in a comforting state, and how the heart may beat gently like a clock ticking during a thunderstorm. We shall discuss salient ideas on how to tap into intuition and how to be in tune with the inner self. This discourse is designed to provide *flashes of wisdom and moments of delight*.

I. Abiding in harmony

Every human being is a bundle of contradictions. At any given moment we are capable of being selfless and selfish, grateful and ungrateful, reasonable and unreasonable, foolish and wise. To be challenged by these opposing tendencies is normal and natural. They are a part of life and part of the human condition.

It is vital not to be torn by inner tension. A clash between career and family interests, for example, could undermine our inner peace and calm. With imagination, however, we can transform our inner tensions into inner harmony. In the midst of a noisy world, we could compose such an inner harmony to carry us into serenity. At these moments, we truly enjoy inner peace and calm.

Similarly, in order for us to have our own inner harmony, we must first cultivate the voices of hope and joy within us and then blend them together with our diverse desires. We become well balanced and well integrated, at peace with ourselves and consequently at peace with others.

Maximize strengths: minimize weaknesses

The more we realize that our strengths outweigh our weaknesses, the more confident and happy we become. There is, naturally, a great array of characteristics that could be deemed as either strengths or weaknesses. First, let us arbitrarily choose four common strengths: selflessness, flexibility, inclusiveness, and empathy. Second, we shall examine the opposing traits as weaknesses: selfishness, rigidity, exclusiveness, and apathy. These concepts together would well illustrate how focusing on our strengths and addressing our weaknesses help us develop a more integrated personality. This is a state more conducive to enjoying inner harmony. Let us examine each pair of traits, beginning with selflessness and selfishness.

Selflessness is a virtue wherein our own interests become secondary to those of others. Selflessness demands sacrifice, and this is not easy. Although some people have risen to great heights of self-denial, most ordinary people are not saints. To augment this strength, we need to test the limits of our sacrifice for others.

To be selfish is easy because it arises from our need for self-preservation. It is normal when we place our interests above those of others. Selfishness often hurts people because we tend to benefit at the expense of others. We must learn to pause and reflect before taking action, so as not to hurt others.

Flexibility is a mark of strength. We must be flexible like the bamboo that bends gracefully with the wind while remaining strongly rooted. Flexibility helps us to adjust to sudden and unpredictable winds of change. Keep your feet firmly planted, and be subtle by turning your head and stretching your arms like the bamboo.

Rigid thinking, flexibility's counterpart, is a mark of a closed mind. In his book *Growing Young*, Ashley Montagu[3] (1905–1999) describes such thinking as "psychosclerosis," which is the hardening of the mind. The free circulation of ideas is restricted, as in arteriosclerosis, in which the free circulation of blood is restricted. To prevent psychosclerosis, we must expose ourselves to new points of view with a willingness to be challenged.

To be inclusive is to be broadminded. With this spirit, we include within our circle of goodwill as many people as possible that differ from us culturally and in their way of thinking. An inclusive spirit tears down fences and builds bridges. "If you are gracious to strangers, regard yourself as a citizen of the world," wrote Pericles[4] (c. 495 BC–429 BC).

An exclusive attitude is a common human failure. People generally rest comfortably within their own circle and are wary of strangers. The ancient

Greeks described this quality as *xenophobia*. To overcome it we need to cultivate the elevated idea that all the earth's peoples belong to the same human family.

In each of us there is a little of all of us

Empathy is rewarding to those who give and receive it. It refers to our capacity to put ourselves in other people's shoes and to appreciate their unique situations. Imagine doing another's job for a day, a job that you would consider unpleasant.

In contrast, apathy appears when we are indifferent to the interests of family, friends, colleagues or the unfortunate and vulnerable. Apathy is a common human failing that shows our insensitivity to things that matter. The poet Dante perhaps exaggerated this point when he wrote, "The hottest places in hell are reserved for those who are apathetic."

Perfect complementary qualities

Although certain attributes are themselves desirable, when combined with complementary qualities they become more powerful. Complementary qualities transform and enrich our personalities. The list of potential qualities in any person is immense, but if we combine reason with passion, courage with caution, and pride with humility, our thoughts and deeds are likely to be balanced and harmonious.

A passionate love for a man or a woman, for instance, is a fantastic experience. It should, however, be balanced with reason, telling us whether that person would be a good marital or romantic partner.

Both courage and caution are desirable qualities. Sometimes living itself is an act of courage, but with too much courage we may display a foolish bravado. On the other hand, with too much caution, we may remain frozen by inaction. William Wordsworth[5] (1770–1850) wrote that "wisdom is often nearer when we stoop than when we soar."

To possess courage and caution to the right degree are marks of wisdom.

Erich Fromm[6] (1900–1980) held the view that the opposite of courage is not caution but conformity. There is a sheep-like quality in some people that makes it difficult for them to think critically. They are not receptive to fresh ideas and resist changes to their way of thinking.

Excess pride is a common human failing, which weakens the power to reason.

It is healthy to have pride in our accomplishments and ourselves. Pride gives us dignity and poise, but when carried to excess, it may push us to be egocentric. Closely associated with pride are stubbornness and narrowness of vision. Even people in high circles are not free of pride.

Conversely, humility adds to our greatness when we recognize our limitations. It does not entail crawling at another's feet. Humility, like pride, should be dignified. As the Bible says, "he that humbleth himself shall be exalted."[7] And Kahil Gibran[8] (1883–1931) expressed the same idea in a poetic way when he stated, "A root is a flower that disdains fame."

A judicious mixture of complementary qualities is conducive to attaining inner harmony that, in turn, is a condition for enjoying inner peace and calm. Achieving these two cherished goals will *give us flashes of wisdom and moments of delight.*

Reconcile reason with passion

Plato, the ancient Greek philosopher, was born in 253 BC. He was like a "walking university," exploring many aspects of human knowledge. He founded a school in Athens for intellectual discussion called "The Academy." This term is still used today to describe institutions of higher learning. Laying the foundation for a good part of our present-day knowledge, his influence is felt to this day.

Plato claimed that all passions are exaggerations; hence, they are called passions. He asserted that the happy man is the disciplined man. Happiness comes to us when our power to reason reigns supreme. Reason restrains our impulses when we act hastily without considering the consequences.

To launch a project without planning is unsound, and to quickly confide in strangers is unwise. Reason rescues us from thoughtless actions that often lead to needless troubles. If we are willing to practice a certain self-restraint, then we may be able to achieve a measure of inner harmony.

Modern psychologists, however, emphasize the importance of emotional enrichment. Giving and receiving emotions, such as love, compassion, empathy, sympathy, care, and understanding, enriches human relationships. It may even be argued that positive emotions are themselves based on sound reason.

Drawing a balance between reason and passion enhances inner harmony. While emotions enrich life, reason acts as a restraining force against excessive emotional reaction. While emotions of love and friendship make life worth living, they need to be balanced by the ability to reason and form good judgments. A kind heart is of little value in chess. In a word, reason should be balanced with passion. Thus, going against reason, one may purchase a luxury home based only on sentiment. The result is an unaffordable home and a lot of stress. In the area of relationships, emotions may rule over reason. A person may fall head over heels in love only to discover that, while love is blind, marriage is an eye-opener.

Reason plays a vital role in controlling our negative emotions, such as anger. With reason we can respond to anger in the right manner, to the right degree, and at the right time. When we fall into inner turmoil because of negative emotions, reason lifts us into a state of inner harmony, where we enjoy inner peace and calm.

A profound and refreshing explanation about the interaction between reason and emotion is presented by Daniel Goleman in his book *Emotional Intelligence*. He claims that personal excellence is best achieved when the ability to think or reason is harmonized with the capacity to develop positive emotions. He asserted that all human behavior is determined both by various levels of intelligence and by various levels of emotional interests. Chief among them are self-awareness, self-discipline, optimism, and empathy, particularly about the needs and fears of others.

Through careful research, Goleman proves that there is a biological basis to the way we think and the way we act emotionally. Two distinct paths of the brain shape our process of thinking and our process of acting emotionally. The Neo Cortex is the center of our thinking faculty, and the Andromeda is the center that shapes our emotions. Our thinking capacity is revealed through our levels of IQ and our emotional reactions through our emotional intelligence (EQ). They include the qualities we mentioned earlier and a display of care and understanding, gratitude, and graciousness to strangers. These sentiments prompted St. Augustine (354–430) to write that a loving heart is the truest wisdom. Goleman's research suggests that, when reason complements emotion, such a combination produces the best results.

This can explain why people with high IQ seem to sometimes fumble when compared with those whose IQ may not rate as high. This is because the second group of people have an edge by being endowed with superior emotional intelligence. Consider this example: a social worker's IQ may be no match to that of a systems analyst. But her qualities of empathy and sympathy may endow her to be a better person. She holds an edge over the systems analyst because of her superior emotional intelligence.

Some businesses have recognized this fact. They are not merely looking for employees with a high IQ and technical expertise but for people with good social skills and sound judgment. What is encouraging about emotional intelligence is that it is malleable. It can be nurtured so that a person grows and blooms to become a fine individual. Businesses also realize that a fine mind may not be a fine soul.

Reconciling reason with passion is one way to achieve inner peace and calm.

Let your inner and outer self be one

Sometimes we are afraid and feel like strangers in a strange world that we never made. This attitude arises from the two sides of our personality—the inner and the outer. The inward side represents our true thoughts and feelings that we keep to ourselves as our private domain. Our outward behaviour is how society views us through our words and actions and is an expression of our inner self. This blending of the two sides of our personality usually depends on circumstances surrounding us. The more they can be reconciled, the more serene we become. On the other hand, the more the two are out of sync, the less harmonious we are.

We face many challenges in life, one of which is how to reconcile the two sides of our personality. It is sometimes daunting to be scrupulous among the unscrupulous, liberal among the illiberal, and tolerant among the intolerant. Conversely, we may find many people who are superior to us in some respects and we need to connect with them.

We may really be much better than what others think of us. It is common for us to judge ourselves by our noble intentions. Others, however, judge us by our actions, which may be less than noble; we need to give our good intentions greater credit.

In balancing the inward and outward sides of our personality, we must jealously guard our privacy, our secrets, and our own turf. This is vital because it gives us an identity and preserves our uniqueness.

We must be careful not to be too secretive in our lives, even though it may be tempting to project a more positive image of ourselves than what is actually true. A master authority on the importance of appearances was Niccolo Machiavelli[9] (1469–1527). He claimed that to be really honest, faithful, and kind would be fatal. What really matters is to appear honest, faithful, and kind. He advised rulers of his day to blatantly assume a double personality—one for private life and the other for the public. He lived in the sixteenth century, but his ideas have had a tremendous impact on successive generations, including our own.

Develop self-esteem

Self-esteem is essential for our happiness and success. It is a spark that ignites our ability to grasp at opportunities, cope with challenges, and be respected for our values and accepted for who we are. High self-esteem allows us "to feel better and live better," according to Nathaniel Branden in *The Six Pillars of Self-Esteem*.

Research reveals that people with high self-esteem are more likely, in the long run, to persevere with difficult tasks. They tend to be more rational and realistic, intuitive, creative, flexible, and independent. They also more readily accept their shortcomings and take steps to correct them. People with low self-esteem, on the other hand, are more prone to give up in the face of difficulty. They are fearful of the new and unfamiliar, are rigid, defensive, or even a little hostile. These traits have been referred to as behavior emanating from an inferiority complex. These people have difficulty in facing failures, give up easily, and leave their problems unsolved.

A person with high self-esteem treats failures as inevitable and moves on diligently until he achieves his goals. He is also ambitious in trying to experience life more fully, intellectually, emotionally, and spiritually. He attracts like-minded people, who nourish his relationships and enrich his personality.

In the area of forming intimate relationships, a healthy self-esteem is a great asset. One becomes more receptive to receiving love and more resourceful in giving love, both of which are a primary human need.

On the other hand, a barrier to romantic happiness is poor self-esteem. This is a state in which one may shy away from forming intimate relationships. Speaking as a layperson, I don't believe that poor self-esteem in healthy.

It is critical that we like ourselves because it becomes easier to like others.

Self-esteem and self-love are interchangeable. There is a mysterious energy in love commencing with those who are near to us and then extending to wider circles. With a loving attitude we lighten the load for others.

Could self-love be excessive? The answer is yes. We could be self-centred like Narcissus[10], the legendary Greek character who was in love with himself. The humorist and playwright Oscar Wilde[11] (1854–1900) expressed a contrary view to this. He wrote that when you are in love with yourself, there are no rivals to your love. It could be the beginning of a long romance.

II. Finding inner contentment

The joyfulness of a man prolongeth his days.
—Ecclesiasticus

Inner contentment is a sort of natural wealth. Thus, a woman with one diamond may be happier than one with two diamonds. A man with a Timex watch may be happier than the one with an expensive Rolex. Happiness consists not in possessing a great deal, but in being content with what we possess. It is not how much we have, but how much of it we enjoy that determines our happiness.

The deepest happiness—and the ultimate source of it—lies in inner contentment. It is a priceless treasure and with it, as Victor Hugo[12] (1802–1885) wrote, "We can see a feast in everything." Silver and gold are desirable only if they strike a chord within us; otherwise, they are like clay. An exotic place will offer little excitement if our heart is restless. Singing, drinking, and dancing will offer few thrills if our heart is not at peace. We may wander the world in search of adventure and romance only to discover upon our return that true happiness resides within ourselves. Without inner contentment, our hearts are restless, though we may possess much. With inner contentment, our hearts are restful, even though we may possess little. Inner contentment is a sure way to enjoy inner peace and calm, which is a principal purpose of life.

A realistic understanding of inner contentment will enable us to recognize that we can never be totally happy all the time. Even if we could achieve total happiness, we would never be able to accept it. St. Thomas Aquinas[13] wrote that "man will never be perfectly happy as long as something remains for him to desire and to seek."

We shall now discuss six conditions that promote inner contentment and how they may serve as an inner sanctuary against the strains and stresses of life.

To thy own self be kind[14]

> *Full wise is he that can himself knoweth.*
> *—Geoffrey Chaucer (1340-1400)*[15]

We should never be too harsh on ourselves, like the cynic who wrote that he had more trouble with himself than with any other person. It is best to measure ourselves by our best moments and not by our worst.

We can further enhance inner contentment by being gracious to ourselves. A courageous admission of our mistakes helps us redress them. With a courageous spirit, we must avoid too much regret over our mistakes and too much remorse over our wrongs. In a constructive way, we could profit from our mistakes and compensate for our wrongs, provided that they are not too serious. In this way, we regain our peace of mind. We would do well to remember the words of Eric Hoffer that "many of the insights of the saint stem from his experience as a sinner."[16]

The thought is comforting that we are not alone in being imperfect. All human beings are imperfect. We are, to various degrees, fair and unfair, wise and unwise, sane and insane, so much so that no two people are alike. Herman Melville (1819–1891)[17] beautifully expressed this idea in his description of rainbows. He wrote that the line where the red tint ends and where the orange tint begins is really not a definitive line. We see the difference of the colors, but where exactly does the first one blend into the other? So is it with sanity and insanity. There is no clear dividing line separating the two states.

A guide to our thinking is to listen to our "inner voice." Although we do not hear it clearly like a spoken word, in many ways it acts in a similar manner, constantly sending us messages. These messages are authentic because our past experiences affect us both consciously and unconsciously in the form of an "inner voice."

Besides savoring the positive experiences of the past, we must employ them to offset the negative experiences of our past. Taking pride in our achievements can erase the frustration of our failures. We must spare ourselves from all troubles that are self-inflicted.

Every human being is an heir to faults and follies. We are therefore not less worthy than others. It would, however, be wise to gradually accept ourselves by accentuating within us all that is positive; self-insight is a valuable asset. Ultimately, we must learn to forgive ourselves, which may enable us to live with ourselves. This is a path to inner contentment.

A little understanding of ourselves would reveal certain aspects of our contradictory nature. Thus, when we are engaged in complex activity, we are yearning for a simple life, but not for too long. We are soon bored and pine for a more challenging life. Similarly, when our days are very hectic, we long for leisure and rest. On achieving these goals, we become restless and hope for the days when we are fully engaged in activity.

I have experienced a minor form of self-deception. In 1991 I wrote a book called *A Global Plan for the Advancement of Humanity*, which provides a blueprint for a better world. Although this document received the support of Nobel Prize winners and the United Nations, the reality dawned on me that achieving the aims of the book was too much of a mammoth undertaking. I learned from this experience not to be harsh on myself for this failure but to rejoice that the *Global Plan* did receive international recognition. I learned to be kind to myself.

Rest your happiness on controllable factors

If a happy life eludes us, happy times may await us. So it is wise to base our inner contentment on firm grounds, over which we have firm control. Love of nature, music, books, and good friends, for example, are all inexhaustible sources of satisfaction.

Nature offers us many pleasures with its infinite variety of scenic beauty. Imagine sitting by the seashore, sipping tea, and watching a sunset, or calmly looking up in the night and admiring Venus shining brightly in the dark sky.

Music offers much to stir the soul with delight. From the symphonies of Beethoven[18] to the melodies of Elvis, from country to world beat, jazz to soul—what rapturous concerts exist to suit every taste. Literature offers us a rich collection of materials, from classics and comics to biographies and best sellers of every kind to transport the mind.

Personal and social relationships offer a wide circle of friends, all with individual and colorful personalities. How rewarding would it be to meet someone like Romeo, bold and romantic, or Desdemona,[19] loving and loyal, or a colleague who has a simple character and a subtle mind. The inner contentment that arises from controllable factors does *present us with flashes of wisdom and moments of delight.*

In contrast, it is unwise to let our inner contentment depend largely on uncontrollable factors. It is frustrating not being able to impact others to the extent that we would like. People have minds of their own and it is difficult to read them; hence, we err in our judgment. Even our children, "though they come from us," as the poet Kahlil Gibran[20] (1883–1931) said, think not like us and act not like us. We try to control life, but often life controls us. Still, life presents many opportunities to shape our future in our own way.

It is also wise not to attempt the impossible. As Confucius[21] (551–479 BC) said, we cannot stop the setting sun, or as Aristophanes[22] wrote, "You cannot teach a crab to walk straight." It is also worth noting that, "There is no good in arguing with the inevitable. The only argument available with an east wind is to put on your overcoat" (James Russell Lowell 1819–1891).[23]

The ideas of Percy Bysshe Shelley[24] and Søren Kierkegaard[25] offer cogent suggestions on how we may better manage our life. Shelley recommended that we "fear not the future and weep not for the past." Kierkegaard asserted, "Life can only be understood backwards, but it must be lived forward."

Transform pain into pleasure

Pain is inevitable, and we must learn the art of arresting it. Like joy and sadness, pleasure and pain are mingled in the same yarn. A tolerance for pain heightens pleasure. Great joys are born out of some pain. The extreme joy a mother experiences in bringing forth her child, for instance, is preceded by extreme pain. Pleasure is deepened and enhanced when a person has survived tedious moments. This principle helps us to make our prized pleasures last longer. We therefore make a mistake if we try to have all our nights as party nights. Pleasure is more a by-product than an end.

The pursuit of pleasure is related to the quest for happiness. A requisite for happiness is to know the source of unhappiness, like worrying needlessly. Sometimes it is the immoderate search for happiness that causes unhappiness, like drinking excessively.

An ancient formula for modern times

"To be content without some of the things we want is an essential part of happiness," wrote Bertrand Russell (1872–1970), the British philosopher and mathematician who was awarded the Nobel Prize for Literature in 1950.

The ancient Greek philosopher Epictetus[26] presented a different perspective. His formula for inner contentment placed a higher priority on goals that are realistic and attainable and a lesser priority on goals that are unrealistic and more difficult to achieve. He did not rule out the latter, but emphasized pursuit of the former. In today's parlance, Epictetus would say that it is good to have dreams, but our feet must be firmly planted on the ground. Thus, a desire to be an artist is a realistic goal, but a desire to be an overnight success is unrealistic.

We can also view the practical wisdom of Epictetus as a balance between needs and wants. Needs refer to our basic requirements for food, clothing, and shelter, which we must satisfy for our survival. Wants refer to our fancied desires, where satisfaction is not crucial, though we may consider it so. Bread is a need, but venison and wine are wants. Water is a need, but champagne is a want. A warm coat is a need, but a mink is a want. Actually, only a mink needs a mink.

To enjoy inner contentment we must solve a paradox in our life. We must endeavor to match our limited resources with our unlimited wants. To do so we must first satisfy our vital needs and then arrange our wants according to an order of priorities.

It helps to remain unmoved by exaggerated advertising. It is essential to concentrate more on thoughts than on things and more on lofty values than on cheap valuables. An escape from commercial pressures puts us in a finer world within this world. In a profound statement, T. S. Eliot[27] (1888–1965) cautioned, "We know too much, and are convinced of too little."

An obstacle to happiness is expecting too much happiness.

Connoisseur or consumer?

It is possible to be happy without leading an austere life. Fine food, wine, and dance add spice to life if we do not go to excess. In the pursuit of acquisitions, we may wonder whether it is better to be a connoisseur or a consumer. A connoisseur has a taste for quality products and services. He chooses them very selectively. A consumer is concerned about utility and price and is attracted by bargains. The important factor here is which one of these choices would give us greater inner satisfaction.

The urge to acquire increasingly more and more is a part of our nature. Human desire is infinite. It is never fully gratified. Man could be restless even in paradise. This point is illustrated in a song called "Constant Craving," by Canadian country singer k. d. lang.[28]

A realization of this truth is critical; learning how to contain our desires is a path to inner contentment.

A crown is no cure for a headache

Imagine wearing a crown of diamonds, emeralds, and sapphires. The crown symbolizes much of what this world has to offer: fame, wealth, and power. Through history, there has always been an intense competition to pursue these three goals, even if it meant trampling on the toes of others. Although highly sought after, the crown has definite limits. It cannot do for you what a simple aspirin can do; it is incapable of curing your headache.

Still, the wish to possess goods is a powerful urge. It stems from the fear of being denied our necessities, and hence a quest for unlimited security.

This point is illustrated in the story of two children who stole food to avert the pangs of hunger. Despite being subsequently rescued and fed, they brazenly continued to steal food. Memories of constant hunger had made a lasting imprint that they couldn't overcome.

Similarly, a question to ponder is why some millionaires, having suffered poverty during their childhood, spend their adult lives aggressively accumulating even more wealth. Part of the answer lies in a never-ending acquisitive urge and another in the fact that a crown is no cure for a headache. In other words, we need spiritual values to sustain us with lasting satisfaction in a materialistic world.

III. Secrets to serenity

Life, like a pendulum, swings between a smile and a tear, joy and sorrow, or ecstasy and agony. While savoring the sweet fruits of life, we must also be willing to taste the harsh reality of its bitter fruits. These might appear in various forms of adversity, such as the decline of health or the loss of a loved one. Painful though this adversity might be, we should not be too perturbed. This is the essence of serenity. It offers a safe harbor against any tempest that may strike us with intense fury. A serene spirit will enhance our inner peace and calm. From this fine state we may spontaneously learn to be more thoughtful, creative, and *acquire flashes of wisdom and moments of delight.*

In the next section, we shall discuss three conditions that could help us dwell in serenity.

From loneliness to togetherness
"Water, water, everywhere, nor any drop to drink," cried the Ancient Mariner when he was shipwrecked on the high seas. Though the cry sounds chilling, they are only words contained in a poem written by Samuel Taylor Coleridge (1772–1834).[29]
In today's troubled world, many an anguished person seems to be crying, like the Ancient Mariner, "I see people, people everywhere, but not one to be my soul mate." It is a paradox of life that we could be lonely in a crowded world and that those people who are near to us may not be dear to us.

To a lonely heart, even a candle is company in a dark room.

Loneliness is an obstacle to serenity. Normal problems appear aggravated when we are lonely. We tend to be more fearful and less cheerful, more withdrawn, and less social.

Actually, no mirror can reflect a lonely heart.

It is a fact of life that others will not fully understand the "real you." It requires wisdom to realize that when we are right, not many people remember, but when we are wrong, few people forget.
We usually judge ourselves by our noble intentions, while other people judge us by our deeds. We are really much better than what others think of us.
Combating loneliness is a key to serenity. Certain measures deserve to be taken to escape from the doldrums and put us in a sublime mood. A serene spirit comes to a person when he is at peace with his "inner life" and his "inner world." This world contains a person's private thoughts, experiences, desires, fears, and feelings. It is a world that is very personal and real to him. A good example of serenity is found in the story of Job in the Bible. When buffeted by a whole range of calamities, Job remained calm and tranquil. He said to

his detractors, "Naked came I out of my mother's womb, and naked shall I return thither: the LORD gave, and the LORD hath taken away."[30]

The secret to serenity lies in our ability to share our inner world with another person or a few selected people. When this occurs, our heart is filled with gladness, leaving little room for loneliness. As Pearl Buck[31] wrote, "The person who tries to live alone will not succeed as a human being. His heart withers if it does not answer another heart. His mind shrinks away if he hears the echoes of his own thoughts and finds no other inspiration."

Something to live for

A humorist remarked that a man's wealth might be superior to the man. The wealth is important because it frees us from the fear of want, which is perhaps the greatest freedom we can enjoy. It is now possible for millions to enjoy this freedom that was denied in earlier times. To attain a high standard of living is a legitimate aspiration. After all, life is short, so why not enjoy it with lots of material possessions?

A relevant question to ask is whether the accumulation of riches is sufficient to provide us with enduring happiness. Is the road to riches alone a sure way to attain inner peace and calm? Impressive evidence suggests that we do need meaningful, non-material, altruistic factors to guarantee our happiness. We require something to live for—a commitment to a worthy cause to which we can devote our energies. We need to be stirred by some idealism to escape from the narrow confines of our own interests. A Tamil proverb states that if you cherish an orphan child, then your own child will prosper. When our interests are broad and we are genuinely concerned about others, our inner satisfaction is enhanced and so is our sense of serenity. When our interests are narrow, we tend to become apathetic, and this sense of apathy weakens sensitivity. An extreme example of apathy is found among hardened criminals. They are failures in life because they completely lack any social values.

Transform stress to strength

William Shakespeare (1564–1616) is one of the greatest playwrights of all time, belonging not just to England but to all humanity. Many expressions in his writings have entered into the English vocabulary. They include witticisms like "brevity is the soul of wit,"[32] "talkers are no good doers," and "words pay no debts." Robert G. Ingersoll[33] (1833–1899) describes Shakespeare as "an intellectual ocean, whose waves touched all the shores of thought. American poet Williams Carlos Williams wrote that Shakespeare was the greatest university of all[34] . In his works, he covers the entire spectrum of human events and emotions than any other writer. For his breadth and depth of imagination, he stands unequalled.

In his play *Hamlet*, Shakespeare elegantly poses the question whether life is worth living in the famous soliloquy: "To be, or not to be: that is the question. Whether 'tis nobler in the mind to suffer the slings and arrows of outrageous fortune, or to take up arms against a sea of troubles, and by opposing end them?"

Tension and anxiety are a part of life, and they will end only in death. Stress is therefore inevitable. It is like a shadow that follows us everywhere; life itself begins with a cry and ends with a sigh.

Stress is normal, and if we could learn to cope with it successfully, we would transform it into inner strength and serenity. To withstand stress we need to be like a strong piece of glass that remains unbroken when rocks are hurled at it.

When a human being has emotional stress, it is possible to adapt and bounce back—it is truly amazing how much stress a person is able to withstand. When a marriage ends or we mourn the loss of a loved one, it may seem like the end of the world; but people do recover and go on to lead normal and happy lives. The stress is transformed into inner strength, enabling a person to acquire a serene outlook on life. It seems that "On the wings of time grief flies away" (Jean de La Fontaine 1621–1695).[35]

A key to this transformation is found in our perception of short- and long-term problems: if we view difficult situations in an exaggerated manner, our stress level will likely be high. If we view them in a measured manner, however, our stress level will be normal.

An opportunity exists to avoid unnecessary stress by capitalizing on an interesting attribute of the brain. Research shows that the brain draws no distinction between a real threat and an imaginary threat. When we worry needlessly, we still suffer the adverse effects of stress. It is therefore critical to perceive problems in a rational manner. To worry about a diagnosis that turned out to be negative or fear a possible layoff would be in vain.

Another way to minimize stress is to consider our obligations, particularly to our family and work, not as burdens but as an important part of life. We learn from plants how they gently bend to bear the weight of their fruits and are flexible to the wind.

A prudent strategy is to look for occasions when stress is positive while learning to manage its negative aspects. Thus, a job does not need to be stressful if the grind of the daily work is considered a challenge instead of a chore. Even dull tasks are satisfying if we have a sense of accomplishment.

When we desire the thrills of adventure, stress is welcome and is even joyful. We like an element of danger because we desire excitement. Riding the rapids or flying solo is risky but exciting. Similarly, looking at life's situations in an adventurous way transforms stress to strength.

The perception that we lack control of our lives is a principal cause for stress. Discovering a measure of control is an effective remedy.

A life of tremendous success may cause high stress if we do not moderate our excess actions. This is particularly true for type A personalities who may accomplish great things only at the cost of harming their health. Our strategy, therefore, is to refine a type A personality by embracing the principle of balance and proportion. We shall see in Chapter 5 that this principle embodies much of what is good in nature and human behaviour.

Turn fears to hope

"The rose is fairest when it is budding new, hope is brightest when it dawns from fear," wrote Walter Scott (1771–1832).[36] Similarly, U.S. President John Kennedy said in one of his inspiring addresses, "Hope shines brightly when it rises out of fear." Whereas fear causes fatigue and undermines our inner tranquility, hope gives us energy and strengthens us.

Fear is a universal emotion and manifests itself in many forms when our security is threatened. Fear comes from uncertainty, and life itself is full of uncertainties.

Hope is a universal feeling of optimism that diminishes our fears. When we are fearful of a harsh winter, hope for the coming spring, with blossoms of red, green, and yellow, cheers us. When we are fearful of the future, hope provides us a vision of brighter days to come. As Ovid wrote, "Our hopes are not always realistic but we must always have hope."

Fear disturbs our inner tranquillity because it exaggerates nonexistent dangers. When one is afraid and alone in the jungle, a bush might appear like a bear and anything that rustles may cause panic. Many of our fears are irrational. As Samuel Taylor Coleridge wrote, "What begins in fear usually ends in folly.[37]" Rollo May cautioned that when people are fearsome, they become rigid in their thinking.

It is advantageous to be cheerful because misfortunes hardest to bear are those that never occurred. A hopeful attitude is therefore soothing to the heart. It elevates our spirits and helps us enjoy inner tranquillity. Hope is a natural human feeling. We look forward to a clear day though the morning is misty, and we plant perennials expecting them to flower again. Even in a desolate place, stars still shine. The Talmud[38] suggests that we should hope for a miracle but not count on it.

It is best to hope for things that are possible and probable. Expecting a lovely baby is a realistic hope. Expecting to win a lottery is an unrealistic hope. We need hope particularly during difficult times when the whole world appears chaotic. We need hope during sickness because impressive evidence reveals that it speeds recovery.

Remember, while there is life there is always hope.

Hope helps us to enjoy inner peace and calm; it also *provides us flashes of wisdom and moments of delight*. Let us also remember that is it always morning somewhere in the world.

Coping with change

Change is dynamic. As Comtesse Diane wrote, "There is often a greater contrast between the same person at two different ages, than between two people of the same age."

Change is the law of life and is inevitable. Immediately after we are born we experience abrupt change, adjusting ourselves from the cosy comfort of our mother's body to this world. From the newborn's perspective, breathing for the first time is a major achievement. This is why the obstetrician gives him a pat on the back to stir him to breathe on his own.

From the womb to the tomb there is no escape from change. We need to accept it not as an unfair condition but as an opportunity to move forward. Yet we fear change because we realize we are vulnerable. We seek security to protect all that is predictable and dependable in our lives. We can never fully control change, but we must learn to cope with it. Here are two techniques to help us adjust to change.

Accept the reality of change

Understanding the nature of change, particularly its pattern and direction, will enable us to react to it better. Physically speaking, all things at all times are in the process of becoming something else. Nothing in the world remains the same. Liquid water is constantly changing either to vapor or ice.

We begin to die the moment we are born, and this law applies to all living things. The ancient Greek thinker Heraclitus[39] (535–475 BC) wrote, "No man can step into the same river twice." The river is constantly flowing, and the waters that touched a man now are not the same waters that touched him a minute ago. Change is reality and reality is change. Accepting this truth enables us to adapt to it gracefully.

Observe subtle change

While change is constant, it remains imperceptible to us. Over time an innocent child may turn out to be a troublesome teenager, or a loving couple may gradually drift apart. These changes occur slowly, but we notice them only when they reach a critical point. Changes that cause decline in health may occur in a subtle manner and escape our attention until one day we are shocked to hear about some ailment. Positive changes also may occur in a subtle manner. We may not quite appreciate how a once unkind person has been transformed into a kindhearted individual.

Just like changing seasons, changes are gradual. As seen in the growth of plants, the transformation from seed to sapling to mature plant is a procession. With slow and deliberate purpose, the seed morphs. Time-lapse photography captures this process very well.

Perception plays an important role in change. After the Indian Ocean tsunami tragedy in late 2004, I found myself being fearful of the ocean. The ocean itself has not changed, but my perception of it has changed. At one time I found the ocean soothing and healing, but now I find it relentless and unforgiving.

Both time and perception are pivotal in coping with change. While time does help to heal some of the negative effects of change, perception must be included to fully complete the cycle of change. If you keep an open mind and learn new coping strategies, your brain forms new pathways that help manage the turbulent effects of change.

Expect the unexpected

Ralph Waldo Emerson[40] (1803–1882) wrote, "Life is a series of surprises." It is therefore wise to leave a wide margin for shocks and surprises. By doing so we may, to some degree, cushion ourselves from the pain of sudden contingencies. While it is impossible to fully anticipate the future, sound preparations must be made to confront unforeseen circumstances. A good example would be to buy full medical coverage for traveling abroad or to keep a special fund to rely on during emergencies. Sometimes when luck smiles on us, we should be ready to seize it—for example, opportunities to make handsome profits in the stock market. Norman Cousins[41] (1915–1990) wrote, "Wisdom consists of the anticipation of consequences."

It is prudent to take ample safeguards against the unpredictability of people. Whether they are friends, associates, or even family members, we cannot always be sure that they will act in a way we expect. To avoid disappointments, we should learn to cope with the fickleness and erratic nature of some people.

Many times what we anticipate may not occur, and what we least expect may occur.

The behavior of people often surprises me. People are generally not as good or bad as they first appear. Coping with this unpredictability, for me, is a major challenge. What do you do with those who renege on their word, for instance? One way I found to tolerate such behavior is to realize that I have also been, at times, unpredictable.

Another way is to obtain satisfaction from the behavior of people who are honest, reliable, and straightforward.

Managing life is possible

We all desire to be architects of our destiny. We want to design our life to meet our unique needs, choices, and preferences. We would like to be able to sing "I did it my way" with Frank Sinatra. We believe this ideal will quiet our restlessness and make us happy.

To fully realize this dream is impossible, but to partially achieve it is possible. A modest quest for fulfilling about half of our dreams is realistic. But before we try to lead the life we like, we must overcome certain obstacles—we must rid ourselves of feelings of hopelessness.

Such a state is serious because it can become a self-fulfilling prophecy and catch us in a trap. So it is essential to break this cycle and view life anew. We must convince ourselves that there is hope and that it is practical to exert some control over our lives. Thinking so can actually cause it to happen.

Dr. Mamta Gautami[42], a Canadian psychiatrist, has some encouraging words on how we may better manage life. According to the Gautami formula, "We actually have more control than we think we have."

Thus, in a hypothetical case, if Mr. Smith were to betray us, we could better confront the problem if we isolated it and treated it objectively. On the other hand, the problem would be exaggerated if memories of past betrayals, which are not relevant to the Smith case, continued to haunt us. Consequently, our control of a situation is weakened when we react to it subjectively by connecting it to similar situations.

The Gautami formula also states, "In any specific situation, only 10 percent of your reaction is due to that particular situation. Ninety percent of the reaction is because of your history, what you automatically assumed from your past experiences. Even if you do not fully explore the 90 percent at that time, knowing about it and putting it away helps you to tone down your reaction at the moment and deal more appropriately with one-tenth of the feelings."[43]

Wisdom demands that we accept the reality that we cannot exert complete sway over our lives. We need to focus our intent on those aspects over which we do have a reasonable impact. In this way, it is possible to exercise a measure of control over our lives and thus keep hope perennially alive.

Dwelling in magnanimity

Aristotle, teacher to Alexander the Great[44] (356 BC–323 BC), was considered one of the greatest geniuses of all time. He was a walking encyclopaedia. The impact of his ideas is still felt today in such diverse fields as logic, poetry, politics, and philosophy. He was a student and later a fellow philosopher of Plato.

To Aristotle, the most important and most beautiful of all virtues was magnanimity. While it is good to love and care for others, magnanimity does something superior. It seeks to increase our resources in order to enhance our capacity to be more generous.

Possessing a magnanimous spirit is a definition of a noble and virtuous character. Why is magnanimity such a magnificent virtue? Aristotle argued that it embraces a host of other virtues. If we are magnanimous, we also display towards our fellow human beings an attitude of respect, goodwill, kindness, gentleness, and, above all, forgiveness.

Charles-Louis de Secondat, Baron de Montesquieu[45], the eighteenth-century French philosopher, wrote that when people are kind and sensitive, they are more likely to be happy, particularly when this happiness is shared.

The "Toronto Appeal," a manifesto written by the author in 1992 and signed by four Nobel Prize winners, stated the following: "In today's world, let the hungry child in Kabul become your child in spirit. Let the poor widow in Sri Lanka become your sister in spirit. Let a hundred flowers bloom within your heart."

A magnanimous spirit opens a passage to inner harmony. An East Indian proverb advocates "if we are truly generous, we can also be truly wise" and that kindness is the greatest wisdom.

IV. Abiding in tranquility

William Blake (1772–1834) was an English poet who at one time collaborated with William Wordsworth, another illustrious poet. He suggested that people should be "like a cistern that contains and a fountain that overflows."[46]

We would do well if our character contains deep understanding and if some of our actions overflow with kindness. We need to realize how precious life is and how critical it is to feed our soul not with passing fancies, but with nourishing food.

Popular sentiment implies that happiness lies in wealth and possessions. This idea is true only up to a point. We certainly need money to satisfy our necessities; otherwise, we would be unhappy. But once our basic needs are met, further increments of money do not lead to further increments of happiness, except marginally.

Ed Diener[47], a University of Illinois psychologist, claims that when people suddenly become rich through a windfall, they do enjoy a thrill and a jolt of happiness. This happiness, however, gradually fades away, becoming a fleeting passage in the span of life. Studies of multimillion-dollar lottery winners show that negativism ranks high among them. They often lose their friends, become isolated, and are troubled by depression, divorce, and suicide. A surprising number of them were also broke soon after winning their windfall.

True to our nature, we desire many things; but once we obtain them, we are not fully satisfied because we still crave for more and better things.

This perpetual urge to acquire increasingly more riches is the principal reason why we are never fully happy in spite of accumulated wealth.

We may seek a way out of this dilemma by borrowing an idea from William Blake. Just as a cistern contains water, our personality should contain the understanding that money cannot buy happiness. We need non-monetary factors, like family and friends, to fill the vacuum left by money.

Blake praised the fountain because it constantly overflows. We can also be like a fountain, overflowing not with water but with kindness. We witnessed this phenomenon in the tsunami tragedy in Southeast Asia on December 26, 2004. An outpouring of generosity spread across the world to help the victims rebuild their lives by feeding the hungry, clothing the naked, constructing homes, and caring for the orphans. Never before had so much magnanimity manifested itself to so many people in so many countries.

An outpouring of kindness is also evident during Christmastime. People experience genuine feelings of love and goodwill toward their families and friends. A spirit of "it is more blessed to give than to receive" prevails during this time.

The need to be kind to our fellow human beings is more urgent today than ever before. Jeffrey Sachs, in his remarkable book *The End of Poverty*, laments that about a sixth of humanity lives in extreme poverty—earning one U.S. dollar a day as defined by the World Bank. Sachs proposes creative solutions for ending world poverty. He reiterates the United Nations' recommendation that the rich countries contribute 0.7 percent of their national income as foreign aid. Only six countries have achieved this target.

Our lives could be more abundant if they were like a fountain overflowing with kindness.

Treasure pleasant moments

Realistically, we cannot always be in a state of inner peace and calm. Interruptions are bound to occur. The rough and tumble of life will force us to climb many hills, descend into many valleys, and leap many hurdles. It is after turbulence, after all, that we best experience tranquillity, like a calm after a storm.

Whether our life is calm or stormy, each day is a little life. It is important to fill the day with happy hours. More crucial, we must seize the moment and savor it because life itself consists of a series of moments. We must cherish our pleasant moments because they form a golden link in the chain of happiness. Zen Buddhism teaches that it is vital to expand great moments of satisfaction. They delight the hours, brighten the day, and add joy to life. As John Masefield[48] (1878–1967) wrote, "The days that make us happy also make us wise." It may be said that we cannot always be happy, but we can certainly enjoy happy moments. It is also true that we remember happy moments better than happy days.

Laughter is a sure way to lift us into a happy mood. It stirs the blood, electrifies the nerves, and at least temporarily banishes all worries.

A comforting spirituality

In a profound statement, Albert Einstein[49] (1879–1955) wrote, "The most beautiful thing we can experience is the mysterious. It is the source of all true art and science."

It would be comforting to our souls to view with wonder the mysterious force that seems to govern the universe. This sense of wonder places us in a serene mood, which provides us with *great flashes of wisdom and moments of delight*. We cannot comprehend this mysterious force, but we may obtain glimpses of it. They are tangible and real and can provide us with intense joy if we reflect upon them.

The problem of evil and the reality of suffering shake our faith in this mysterious force, but we can be inspired by nature's beauty.

Fyodor Dostoevsky (1821–1881),[50] the famed Russian novelist, perhaps had these thoughts in mind when he said, "Beauty can save the world." He saw beauty not only in the high heavens but also within the hearts of loving people. Look at the cases of exceptional love among spouses and between parents and children.

We further experience serenity and deep spirituality when we marvel at the beautiful designs of nature. Who painted the distinct stripes on a white horse to give us the zebra? Who gave the peacock its breathtaking plumage? Who adorned Saturn with rings of heavenly splendor? Literary critic Northrop

Frye, who wrote, "The rational design that nature reflects is in the human mind only," expressed one viewpoint. Emmanuel Kant also clarified this idea in the eighteenth century, which we shall discuss in detail in Chapter 2.

A Heavenly Splendor

The bounty of nature is amazing. What an abundance of fruit, grain, and greens the earth presents for our daily sustenance. There seems to be a "benign force" that enriches the soil and helps the plants to grow and reproduce. We observe a glimpse of this "mystic force" in the vast panorama of vegetation. Seeds of all kinds seem to possess a hidden power that is more wondrous than any precious stone. An acorn, if thrown to the ground and discarded for years, will germinate miraculously and grow into a mighty oak. What gives it this innate ability? A plum contains only one seed, but this one seed has the potential to grow into a tree that bears fruit a hundredfold.

One could argue that a sense of spirituality lies deep within the hearts and minds of people. From very early times, human beings have been fascinated by the phenomenon of a mysterious force, one that was not exactly knowledgeable but yet captured their imagination. It is true the world is riddled with superstition and absurd beliefs, but in the midst of them all, there is a humble faith in this mysterious force among a good part of humanity.

Although dogmas and false gods have inflicted much harm on humanity, the belief in a benign force has done mankind much good. Just as gold nuggets are found in the midst of clay, truth is found in the midst of error. It is like a light that shines in whatever lamp it burns.

Call this light God, Brahma[51] providence, nature, or any other name—this light remains a source of great spiritual comfort to millions. Gottfried Leibniz (1646–1716)[52] explained that truth seldom reveals itself in pure form but lies hidden among myths and rituals.

Let compassion prevail

> *As for a future life, every man must judge for himself*
> *between conflicting vague probabilities.*
> —*Charles Darwin*

These probabilities include the idea of rebirth in Buddhism and the idea of heaven in Christianity. Life is a mystery. Today, thousands of babies will be born and thousands will die. From where have these babies come and where have these people gone? The music of Mozart[53] (1756–1791) enchants us and the writings of Shakespeare[54] fascinate us. But where have they gone? Still more pertinent is the question, "Where are we going?" Is there a life after death, and will our good deeds ever be rewarded?

There are no clear answers to these questions except through religion based on faith. People devoutly search for meaning through diverse religious traditions, but they are seldom fully satisfied. These traditions do not offer a genuine dialogue on the purpose of life in a true ecumenical spirit. The various groups remain largely compartmentalised.

What is most needed today is compassion to understand the deep spiritual crises facing people. Much of our restlessness, even in the midst of plenty, is rooted in this spiritual crisis, and we need a lot of compassion to address it.

One eminent thinker who wrestled with this spiritual crisis was Johann Goethe,[55] the nineteenth-century German philosopher. He spent most of his life, from age twenty-five until about seventy-five, pondering the purpose of life. His ideas are reflected in his masterpiece, *Doctor Faust*. Goethe claimed that the purpose of life lies in the meanings we attach to life. The pursuit of power or pleasure, or the practice of virtue, will dictate the type of life we lead. Life is like a journey, and we must do our best to get the utmost out of our brief sojourn on earth. During this journey, let compassion prevail.

The Eight-Fold Noble Path

From his origins in India, Gautama Buddha's message of sublime hope has inspired billions of people for more than 2,000 years. To Buddha, one of the realities of life was suffering. An escape from this plight was possible by adopting an enlightened attitude, one of which was the doctrine of impermanence. Everything in this world is changing. Nothing is permanent; eventually, all things pass away.

What seems to be the stability of appearances is really an illusion. Buddha referred to the state of things not as "being" but as "becoming," a constant shifting and rearrangement of the parts. Wisdom lies in our ability to cope with impermanence. We must learn to remain calm and serene in the midst of a changing world. One way to achieve this is through the practice of universal compassion. Buddha described it as a form of loving-kindness that extends to all human beings without distinction. This kindness offers comfort to all humanity because suffering is their common lot. We must nurture it and allow it to fill the soul until we reach a state of inner bliss called "nirvana" or "nibbana." According to Buddha, this is the ultimate purpose of life.

We should strive to achieve inner serenity through the eight-fold noble path as suggested by Buddha. The eight elements of the path are:

1. Right thinking
2. Right ideas
3. Right desire
4. Right language
5. Right attitude
6. Right effort
7. Right action
8. Right livelihood

We must first engage in "right thinking." If we champion a noble cause, we also become noble-minded. Right thinking gives us the right ideas and desires, and together they will help us engage in right actions. To engage in right thinking means to reflect about life through a process of regular meditation. Great are the rewards for those who practice it faithfully. The promising thing is that everyone is able to meditate because it is so simple and natural.

Through right thinking, the mind generates right ideas, like a capacity to distinguish between good and evil. Sublime thoughts make a sublime person and are a key to enjoying inner peace. To Buddha, we are made of something more than just flesh and blood. *We are what we think.* The essence of a person is the way he thinks and the ideas he holds, which determine his personality entirely. Basically, different ideas are what distinguish people from one another, not physical attributes. People who possess noble ideas will display noble characters.

Right desires emanate from intense reflection. The golden rule according to Buddha is to be moderate in all our desires; the constant craving within us must be contained. One way to do it is through acts of generosity. Right language lies in abstaining from lying, abusive words, and idle chatter. A right attitude is essential for a true understanding of life. One should, to a fair degree, make a right effort, that is exert oneself to achieve fruitful results.

Right action is the end result of practising the above three steps. In essence, it leads to a life of universal compassion. It is important to know what is right and to do what is right.

Finally, for right livelihood, earn your living through honest means.

The soothing effects of meditation

Blaise Pascal[56] (1623–1662) eloquently wrote, "All the trouble in the world is due to the fact that men cannot sit still in a room." Meditation calms us. It is a technique for following the Noble Eightfold Path. Meditation has been practiced in India for more than two thousand years. It is not a chore or fad but a proven mental technique for achieving relaxation. While we shall discuss the techniques of meditation later, here we shall explore the psychological reasoning underlying it. Just as the body needs rest, the mind also needs rest. Sleep and other forms of relaxation offer relief from physical stress. The mind, however, requires a deeper kind of rest to relieve it from mental and emotional stress. Sleep, though helpful, cannot offer this type of psychic relief.

Meditation is a technique that is soothing to the mind not when it is asleep, but when it is awake. This is the striking characteristic of the practice. It is a higher form of rest, akin to the brief "rest" in a symphony. A rest is a part of the score that heightens the music and makes it more melodic.

The mind also has been compared to a monkey that is forever restless; tying it down would be impossible. But offering some fruit to the monkey might make it quiet. Meditation is the fruit for the restless mind.

For maximum benefits, one should meditate twice a day, in the morning and in the evening, for about twenty minutes each time. Commence your exercise by sitting comfortably in a chair or on a bed, with your eyes closed, feeling your breath. Be fully conscious of inhaling and exhaling the air through the nostrils, passing down the throat to the lungs, and to the abdomen. Try to keep thoughts away. If they come, do not resist them. Gradually, they will fade away.

Through regular meditation, your mind could eventually reach a high state of rest that would be very refreshing. It is likely to remain calm and serene even amid turmoil. Just as water mirrors the sky only when it is tranquil, the mind truly reflects its insights only when it is serene.

In conclusion, here is an edited version of "Desiderata,"[57] which seems to complete the foregoing ideas:

> Go placidly, amid the noise and haste and discover your peace in silence. Without surrender, be on good terms with all persons.
>
> Speak your truth quietly and clearly and listen to others, even the dull and ignorant; they too have their story.
>
> Be not cynical about love, for in the face of all apathy and harshness it is as perennial as the grass.
>
> Take kindly the counsel of the years, gracefully surrendering the things of youth.
>
> Nurture strength of spirit to shield you in sudden misfortune. Do not distress yourself with worries. Many fears are born of fatigue and loneliness.
>
> Control yourself, but also be gentle with yourself. You are a child of the universe, no less than the trees and the stars; you have a right to be here.
>
> And whether or not it is clear to you, the universe is unfolding as it should. Therefore, be at peace with God, whatever you conceive Him to be.
>
> Whatever the labor and aspirations in the noisy confusion of life, keep peace with your soul—with all its sham, drudgery, and broken dreams, we still live in a beautiful world.

Paradoxes to ponder

> A man there was and they called him mad;
> The more he gave the more he had.[58]
> --John Bunyan

> Men are cruel, but man is kind.
> --Rabindranath Tagore

> A life of ease is a difficult pursuit.
> --William Cooper

> It is not good to have all one wants.[59]
> --Blaise Pascal

> There must be more to life than having everything.
> -- Maurice Sendar

> It is not good to have too much liberty.
> It is not good to have all one wants.
> -- Blaise Pascal

1. This book has been a labor of love. While writing it I dipped my pen in the ink of suffering.
2. An American writer, philosopher, and longshoreman. He was self-educated and came to fame in the 1950s with the publication of his first book, The True Believer. Eric Hoffer, The Passionate State of Mind (Harper, 1955), 8.
3. A British anthropologist and humanist who popularized issues such as race and gender and their relation to politics and development. Ashley Montagu, Growing Young (Praeger/Greenwood, 1989).
4. A prominent and influential statesman, orator, and general of Athens in the city's Golden Age
5. The poet Wordsworth was credited with ushering in the English Romantic Movement with the publication of Lyrical Ballads (1798) in collaboration with Samuel Taylor Coleridge. William Wordsworth, The Poetical Works of William Wordsworth (Phillips, Sampson and company, 1856), 82.
6. An internationally renowned Jewish-German-American social psychologist, psychoanalyst, and humanistic philosopher.
7. Luke 14:11, KJV
8. A Lebanese poet and artist. His work is notable for its use of formal language and insights on topics of life using spiritual terms
9. Born in Florence, Italy, Machiavelli was well known as a political philosopher, musician, poet, and romantic comedic playwright. He is best known for his work called The Prince (1532), in which he boldly claimed that the end justifies the means.
10. He so admired his image in the water that he fell into it and drowned
11. An Anglo-Irish playwright, novelist, poet, and short story writer, Wilde was best known for his barbed and clever wit. He was imprisoned for his homosexual behavior.
12. A French poet, artist, and dramatist. A recurrent theme in his writing was humanity's eternal struggle in confronting the problem of evil
13. Aquinas was an Italian monk and philosopher who lived from 1225 to 1274. He attempted to find evidence of God or intelligent design without recourse to any supernatural revelation. Thomas Aquinas, A Summa of the Summa: The Essential Philosophical Passages of St. Thomas (Ignatius Press, 1990), 381.
14. In Shakespeare's Hamlet, Polonius suggests to his son Laertes, "To thine own self be true."
15. An English author, poet, philosopher and diplomat, Chaucer is often referred to as the father of English literature. He was most famous for writing The Canterbury Tales. Geoffrey Chaucer, The Canterbury Tales: Being Selections from the Tales of Geoffrey Chaucer (Chapman and Hall, 1884), 159.
16. Eric Hoffer, The Passionate State of Mind (Harper, 1995), 11
17. Melville, the author of Moby-Dick, was largely considered a failure during his lifetime, but was "rediscovered" in the 20th century when his novel was accepted as a literary masterpiece.

18. Beethoven was a genius but a humble man. He wrote about himself that, "Beethoven can write music, but he cannot do anything else."
19. In Shakespeare's "Othello," she was the heroine who remained ever faithful.
20. An artist, poet, and writer who was born in Lebanon and spent much of his productive life in the United States
21. A Chinese thinker and social philosopher whose teachings have deeply influenced East Asian life and thought.
22. His life straddled two centuries. He lived from 446 to 388 BC and was a Greek comic-dramatist. He is also known as the Father of Comedy and the Prince of Ancient Comedy.
23. An American Romantic poet, critic, satirist, writer, diplomat, and abolitionist. James Russell Lowell, The Writings of James Russell Lowell, (Riverside Press, 1890), 17.
24. During his short life (1792–1822), the English poet wrote many beautiful lyrics and love poems. He formed a friendship with Byron, the English poet. Shelley died an untimely death in Italy.   Percy Bysshe Shelley, The Complete Works of Percy Bysshe Shelley (Virtue & Company, 1904),337.
25. A Danish philosopher and theologian (1813–1855). Søren Kierkegaard, Kierkegaard, (Cassel, 1955), 19.
26. This first-century Greek philosopher is the father of Stoicism, a school of philosophy that applauded courage in confronting the struggles of life.
27. This poet, dramatist, and literary critic received the Nobel Prize for Literature in 1948. Thomas Stearns Eliot, Selected Essays (Harcourt, Brace , 1950), 32.
28. On her father's side she is of German and Icelandic origin, and on her mother's side, of Russian-Jewish origin.
29. Coleridge was an English poet, philosopher and critic. Samuel Taylor Coleridge, Ancient Mariner (Sampson Low, 1857), 18.
30. Job 1:21, KJV
31. A twentieth-century American writer who won the Nobel Prize for literature, Buck was best known for her work The Good Earth.
32. From Hamlet.
33. An American civil war veteran, political leader, and orator.
34. http://www.sas.upenn.edu/sasalum/newsltr/spring99/Shakespeare.html Penn Arts and Sciences, Spring 1999.
35. Generally regarded as the most famous French writer and poet of the seventeenth century.
36. Recognized as a prolific Scottish historian, novelist, and poet popular in Europe during his time. Many of his works remain as classical English literature. Walter Scott, The poetical works of Walter Scott (Robert Cadell, 1820), 149.
37. Samuel Taylor Coleridge, The Complete Works of Samuel Taylor Coleridge: With an Introductory Essay (Harper & Brothers, 1853)
38. The Talmud is a record of rabbinic discussions pertaining to Jewish law, ethics, customs, and history.
39. His writings had an influence on Plato and Socrates.

40. Ralph Waldo Emerson, The Works of Ralph Waldo Emerson (G. Bell & sons, 1906), Emerson was an American essayist and poet.
41. Cousins was a prominent political journalist, author, professor, and world peace advocate
42. Gautami, IRONDOC: Practical Stress Management Tools for Physicians, Book Coach Press, p.63 She is a Fellow of Good Standing with the Royal College of Physicians and Surgeons of Canada.
43. Gautami, p.45.
44. Alexander the Great was the most successful military commander in history. Before his death, he conquered most of the world known to the ancient Greeks, never losing a battle.
45. He is famous for his theory on The Separation of Powers. Many constitutions the world over are based on this theory as a safeguard to ensure liberty and democracy.
46. June Singer, William Blake, The Unholy Bible: A Psychological Interpretation of William Blake. Published by Putnam for the C. G. Jung Foundation for Analytical Psychology, 1970, 101.
47. Author of Well-being: The Foundations of Hedonic Psychology. New York: Russell Sage Foundation, 2003.
48. An English poet laureate. John Masefield, The Poems and Plays of John Masefield (The Macmillan company, 1922), 67.
49. A German-born theoretical physicist, Einstein is widely considered one of the greatest scientists of all time. He is best known for the theory of relativity (specifically mass-energy equivalence, $E=mc2$). Albert Einstein, The Joys of Research (Smithsonian Institution Press, 1981), 78.
50. Born in Moscow, Dostoevsky was imprisoned in Siberia for four years for his compassionate political views. His novels, which often feature characters living in poor conditions with disparate and extreme states of mind, explore human psychology while analyzing the political, social, and spiritual states of the Russia of his time.
51. A Sanskrit word for "God.".
52. He invented the binary system, which is the foundation of virtually all modern computer architectures.
53. Mozart was a prolific and influential composer of the classical era. His creation of more than six hundred compositions includes works widely acknowledged as pinnacles of symphonic, concert, chamber, piano, operatic, and choral music.
54. According to Alexander Pope, Shakespeare seems to have known by intuition, to have looked through nature at one glance.
55. Goethe also was a poet, novelist, dramatist, humanist, scientist, theorist, and painter.
56. A French mathematician, physicist, and religious philosopher, Pascal was a child prodigy who was educated by his father. His earliest work was in the natural and applied sciences, where he made important contributions to the construction of mechanical calculators.

57. Written in 1933 as part of a personal Christmas greeting by Max Ehrmann, who lived in Indiana. He died in 1945.

58. John Bunyan (1628–1688), an English Christian writer, wrote The Pilgrim's Progress, arguably the most famous published Christian allegory.

59. Blaise Pascal, Thoughts, (Cosimo Inc. 2007), p. 127

Chapter 2
Give Yourself a Dazzling Mind

Chapter 2
Give Yourself a Dazzling Mind

The human mind is infinitely richer than any gold mine. The mind embraces the vast universe, peers into an atom, composes melodious music, and designs a plane that can fly faster than the speed of sound.

While it is true that animals are able to think to some degree, the power of the human mind is infinitely superior. Our brain stores knowledge and uses the information whenever it is needed. In a sense, we are walking libraries.

Nimbleness is an extraordinary feature of our mind. Within seconds, it can shift its focus from one phenomenon to another: from answering a simple question to the working of a complex crossword puzzle, playing an easy game of cards to a challenging game of chess. The mind is indeed very nimble.

In this chapter we shall discuss many ways to give ourselves a dazzling mind and explore how to achieve our real potential. Because the mind is a single entity, the following points are interrelated and reinforce one another. I hope this discussion will enable you to acquire *flashes of wisdom and moments of delight*.

A diamond with many facets will shine brilliantly. Similarly, the mind will shine best when its many facets can radiate with the light of reason. It is objective and subjective, or scientific and artistic. It is able to glow with its latent power and be luminous about reality in a dark world of doubt and error. In a word, the mind is a gift endowing us with a divine quality. Let us examine its leading features.

I. Cultivating a sense of proportion

For some people, a primary goal in life is to enjoy its treasures, such as beauty, goodness, harmony, and wisdom. These qualities have balance and symmetry and show little or no trace of excess. If they are tainted by extremes or become disproportionate, they acquire opposite characteristics; for example, when distorted, beauty turns to ugliness, goodness to evil, harmony to disharmony, and wisdom to folly. Cultivating a fine sense of proportion in our thoughts and deeds is key to attaining a dazzling mind. This way of thinking provides us rich insights and perfects our judgment.

Balance and proportion are found abundantly in nature. Notice the beautiful geometrical patterns of snowflakes or the majestic display of colors in a rainbow. The multicellular pattern of a honeycomb and the intricate design of a maple leaf also show symmetry in nature. Over the centuries, artists have embodied this symmetry into their works by freely imitating patterns found in nature.

Discern beauty in flowers

> *Anyone able to see beauty in every age of life remains young at heart.*
> *—Kafka[60] (1883–1924)*

In most cultures, flowers fulfill people's need for aesthetic satisfaction by conveying messages of love and comfort. They also provide a source of adornment. In fact, flowers are specially designed to appear lovely. While their beauty manifests itself in an infinite variety of ways, the essence of their beauty lies in balance and proportion. There are fine symmetrical patterns and combinations of colors found in lilacs, daisies, pansies, tulips, and marigolds. They flutter gracefully in the breeze in a blaze of glory.

In the sunflower, beauty is enhanced through numbers. The many cone-shaped petals form a nice circle held together by the pistil.

The beauty of the sunflower is enhanced through numbers.

Flowers represent only one aspect of the rich beauty of this world. The hours you spend with your mind absorbed with beauty are hours conducive for your mind to be more imaginative.

Perceive beauty in stone

Rodin's[61] (1840–1917) sculpture called *The Kiss* is an artistic marvel. It exemplifies in perfect form the principle of balance and proportion. An elegant symmetry is seen in the natural contours of the bodies of the lovers. The man's sexual passion is shown in the tension of his right hand. The loving embrace of the woman matches his passion.

With amazing skill, Rodin used light and shadow to display the masculine and feminine features of the lovers. While the man's body appears rough, the woman's body is soft, creating an impression of realism. By sculpturing elegant balances in the muscles and sinews, Rodin was able to make the lovers in stone appear "more real than real." The poet Rainer Maria Rilke (1875–1926)[62] considered the sculpture such a masterpiece that the delight of the lovers' kiss is expressed all over their bodies. She said it is like "a sun that rises and its light is everywhere."

Admire architecture

Symmetry that is pleasing to the eye is seen in fine architecture, such as the Pyramids and the Taj Mahal. They are examples of imposing structures that have elements that relate to each other.

Egyptian pyramids have given inspiration for more than four thousand years.

Egyptian pyramids have given inspiration for more than four
thousand years

The Taj Mahal, in Agra, India, is perhaps the most elegant tomb ever built.

For more than four thousand years the pyramids in Egypt have inspired architects and artists to imitate their simple design. The structures embody the principle of beauty in simplicity and their elegant symmetrical form with four identical sides, which can be seen from outer space.

Buckminster Fuller[63] (1895–1983) described fine architecture as "frozen music." As music is a harmony of sounds, so architecture is a harmony of shapes. Consider Frank Gehry's[64] Walt Disney Concert Hall in Los Angeles—the sweeping shapes of the structure almost seem to reflect the melodies that emanate from within.

Marvel at the symmetry of the human body

Natural beauty exists in the human body. It has bilateral symmetry, with the two sides of the body being alike (see diagram below).

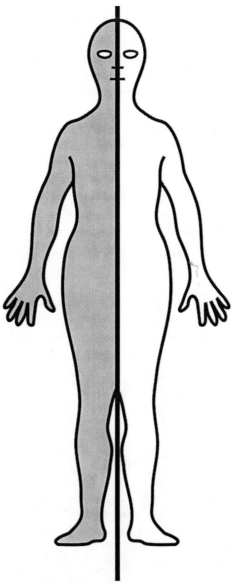

The left and right sides of the human body are mirror images of each other.

These natural body contours and proportions have been a source for much artistic expression. They also have even been reduced to mathematical values often equated with the ratio Phi.

The faces of men and women expressed in idealized sculptures show features that are well arranged. Though ordinary human bodies cannot match the exquisite beauty of the Greek mythological figures Venus and Adonis, we can still accept our own physical appearance. The use of symmetry and proportion to illustrate beauty is a universal occurrence, found in all world cultures.

Another fine example of elegant symmetry is seen in a pair's figure skating performance. In carefully choreographed programs, the skaters complement each other as they jump, twist, and skate gracefully to the music.

Symmetry is also found in duality that is inherent in people. Humanity is good and bad, beautiful and ugly, profound and shallow. A plane dividing a body in half vertically specifies the geometric duality in the external appearance. The left and right halves look alike in the sense that when reflected through a plane, each becomes the other.

The divine proportion

Phi, also known as the Golden Ratio, is a number obtained when a line is divided so that the ratio of the length of the whole line to the length of the larger segment is equal to the ratio of the larger segment to the smaller. This value is found in nature, architecture, and art. It is approximately 1.6180339.

A — — — — — — — — — — — — — — — — B

$$\frac{A + B}{A} = 1.618 \qquad \frac{A}{B} = 1.618$$

An example of this ratio relating to the human body is the lengths of the hand and forearm. The ratio of the forearm and hand (A + B) to forearm (A) is exactly the same as the ratio of forearm (A) to the hand (B).

See diagram below.

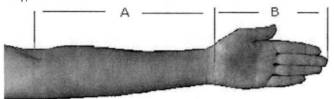

Treasure wisdom

While this entire book pertains to wisdom in a general way, here we shall discuss the quality of wisdom specifically.

To some degree we all seek wisdom. No one is born "wise," and no person is wise all the time. Wisdom is acquired, and it teaches us to take a balanced view of life. We often realize that some of our actions may not bring us happiness, yet we do them anyway.

Samuel Taylor Coleridge asserted that wisdom lies in possessing "common sense to an uncommon degree."[65] Francis Bacon[66] (1561–1626) wrote that wisdom lies "in making more opportunities than one finds." Thomas à Kempis[67] (1380–1471) claimed, "Wisdom comes through suffering." Henry David Thoreau[68] (1817–1862) wrote that the chief characteristic of wisdom is not to do desperate things, and William James[69] (1842–1910) asserted that the art of being wise is the art of knowing what to overlook.[70]

Ralph Waldo Emerson described wisdom in a graphic way. He claimed that Raphael painted it, Shakespeare wrote about it, Martin Luther preached it, George F. Handel composed it, and James Watt mechanized it.

A lot of good things accompany wisdom. At times we know what to overlook and how to distinguish between good and evil. In the Bible, the book of Job states that "the price of wisdom is above rubies."[71] In the fifth-century BC, Sophocles wrote, "Wisdom is a treasure, but its riches need not be embarrassing." The ancient Greeks affirmed that wisdom outweighs wealth and, without it, wealth may be worthless. We saw an example of this lack of wisdom when a recent lottery winner from Ontario fell into poverty after squandering all of the prize money.

When endowed with wisdom, the mind becomes luminous like radium. So while appreciating the immense diversity of mankind, we also discover the oneness and composite nature of humanity. Deep probing may be necessary to comprehend the complex behaviors of people.

Wisdom sharpens our understanding of life. By comparing what we have with what we think we *deserve*, we tend to be happy. On the other hand, we are likely to be unhappy if we do not have what we *desire*. Moreover, we appreciate the fact that no pleasure is lasting unless there is variety in it—even a sweet melody loses its allure when heard too often.

Wisdom also makes us more perceptive, providing us with a "sixth sense." As John Milton[72] (1608–1674) wrote, "It is the unseen wind and not the lofty sails that moves the ship." And Thomas Carlyle[73] (1795–1881) claimed, "Wisdom is the highest achievement of man."

Personally, I have some words of practical wisdom. To flee from folly, is to me, the essence of wisdom.

Appreciate goodness

"In goodness there are all kinds of wisdom," wrote Euripides.[74] Likewise Haveah More said, "Goodness heightens beauty, and it is also a part of reality." W. H. Auden[75] (1907–1973) stated, "Goodness is easier to recognize than to define."

The essence of goodness is seen in a host of virtues. The characteristics of these virtues are discerned in their display of proportion and balance. Ideals are good and true if they tend to be balanced by avoiding extremes. Thus, courage is a noble quality because it lies in the middle of two extremes—cowardice and rashness. In the former, a person may fear circumstances that should not be feared; in the latter, a person rushes into dangerous situations without thinking about the consequences.

To be critical is good because it refines our judgment. Critical thinking lies somewhere in the middle between being gullible, as in believing propaganda, and being cynical, as in looking both ways before crossing a one-way street.

The avoidance of extremes is unique to goodness and wisdom; for example, a mother loves each of her children in a unique way. Her goodness does not flash; it glows. Goodness, like greatness, is not a means but an end.

William James suggested that we should be humble regarding our perception of the good. The whole of what is good is not revealed to any one person, though each person may grasp some particular aspect of what is good and true. Hence, even prisons and hospitals may have their own special versions of what is good. Thus, some might consider it good to first marry and then have sex. Others might find it good to first have sex and then marry. Each side has a valid point.

A cynical view of human nature was theorised by Thomas Hobbes[76] (1588–1679), the English philosopher. He claimed that man was mainly motivated by selfish interest.

Even when there is altruism, beneath it lie selfish intentions. The chief characteristics of man are pride, avarice, ambition, and fear of death. Reason is a slave to passion, though men are capable of reasoning. Without any social constraints, in a natural state, the lives of men are "solitary, poor, nasty, brutish, and short," Hobbes wrote in *Leviathan*.

Hobbes' view, though influential, has been severely criticized as extreme. Humanity surely has noble qualities and is capable of displaying lofty levels of compassion, friendship, fellowship, and sacrificial love. There is a sound body of evidence to support the belief in the innate goodness of people.

We cannot, however, escape from the reality of evil. Evil does not exist in itself, but is an imperfect reflection of the good; hatred is only a form of frustrated love.

Searching for the truth

Homer[77] saw a connection between wisdom and truth when he wrote, "Wisdom never lies."

A human being is a complex creature who displays a wide range of virtues and faults. As Francis Bacon wrote, "To say that man is a compound of strength and weakness, light and darkness, smallness and greatness is not to indict him but to define him."[78] To gather any truth about his behavior, we need to examine his actions, with a sense of balance and proportion.

Natasha, for example, is an interesting person who is generally honest but not entirely. She is intelligent, warm, and friendly, but frequently she is unwise and moody. She is faithful as well as flirtatious, well organized but sometimes too much so. The truth about Natasha's character lies in taking a balanced view of it, by not exaggerating her assets or shortcomings. Truth, like beauty, eschews any form of excess. It is this intimate connection that prompted John Keats[79] to write, "Beauty is truth, truth beauty—that is all ye know on Earth, and all ye need to know."

II. Tapping the mind's latent powers

We can further enrich the mind by stimulating its innate power. Some of the mind's power may be lying hidden within our intuition and imagination. Immanuel Kant[80] (1724–1804), a thinker who wrote extensively about this, asserted that our latent mental powers are an invaluable source for our conscious mental activities. This innate ability of the mind is abundantly clear among children: they effortlessly grasp new knowledge as if they were previously aware of it.

Try this experiment with some young children. Show the children the figures below and, without any explanations, give each child a pencil. Some of them will probably complete at least one of the figures, proving the point that basic geometrical patterns are innate to the human mind.

Are basic geometric objects innate?

This innate power is also seen if we present an upside-down picture to children. Without being taught, they will reverse the picture into the correct viewing position.

A composite view broadens the mind

Mount Everest, the world's highest peak, can be viewed from many angles, each revealing one true aspect to us. However, a composite picture with many angles would show us the true glory of the mountain. Likewise, it is only by understanding people from different perspectives that we acquire a richer understanding of them—an awareness that dazzles the mind.

An anthropological view of people is fascinating because it helps us to appreciate the gift of the human mind. The brain has reached its present state after millions of years of progressive development. This is evident when we compare the smaller brain size of earlier hominoids (early man) to the average brain size of people today. Evidence suggests that our ancestors were less intelligent. This advanced state of the brain in modern humans applies to the whole human race, though there are vast differences in levels of intelligence.

Our social behavior is a paradox. While people often cannot live without one another, they also find it difficult to live with one another. It is astonishing how much conflict and cooperation exists simultaneously in society today. While these two forces are always interacting, the well-being of society depends on which force is more dominant.

In addition, the political attitudes of people are sometimes contradictory. Bruce is a politician who speaks honestly, but the voters reject him. In contrast, Bryce speaks numerous half-truths, yet he is charismatic and attracts voters like a magnet.

It is also interesting to note that in many societies the wealthy classes are also the governing classes. The idea that money "talks" seems to be almost universally true.

An idea worth reflecting on is psychologist Carl Jung's[81] (1875–1961) concept of an inferiority complex.[82] He claimed that there is a subtle urge among people to feel equal or a little superior to others in some respect. When people lack this conviction, they are troubled because they feel inferior. Some historians attribute Napoleon's extraordinary quest for power to feelings of insecurity because of his short stature. In many of our own actions, we want to accomplish something significant, but this is not always easy. It is comforting to know that anyone could be great because anyone is able to be kind, and kindness is a mark of wisdom.

Philosophically, our mind will be enriched if we take a balanced view about the human condition. It's true that there is much human evil in the world today that causes much human misery, but there is also a lot of goodness. Good and evil exist side by side because human beings are prone to both of them. While the pessimists overemphasize the darker side of people, optimists see the brighter side. The mind of a child, for instance, is malleable and impressionable, which allows society to guide him to become a good human being.

An eclectic or many-sided view of society is indeed stimulating to the mind and provides us with *flashes of wisdom and moments of delight.*

Clear thinking can be yours

Just as a carpet shows a certain design, our mind also displays unique patterns of thinking. These patterns could be broadly divided into two categories—rational and irrational. The former refers to conclusions based on fact that can be easily proved. Two examples of a rational conclusion are the principles that light travels in straight lines and that parallel lines never meet.

An ability to form rational categories empowers the mind to think clearly. Thus, we can reason that power corrupts and that mysteries are not necessarily miracles.

Irrational categories are opinions that may contain only an element of truth but are generally accepted as true. They assume the character of sweeping generalizations, such as the belief that all the ideas of young people are merely kid's stuff and that all ideas of old people are old-fashioned.

Somerset Maugham[83] (1874–1965), in a witty statement, engaged in irrational categorization when he wrote, "The Tasmanians, who never committed adultery, are now extinct." Though it is historically true that they did become extinct, their passing was due to a fatal epidemic.

Goethe wrote that it is easier to perceive error than to find the truth. The former lies on the surface and is easily seen, while the latter lies in depth, where few are willing to search for it.

Gilbert Chesterton[84] (1874–1936) claimed that people who are likely to be bigoted are those who have few convictions, and La Fontaine asserted that the world is full of people who are not wise enough.

Forming rational categories is not easy because it requires time and effort to think clearly. Certain opinions are often arrived at only after considerable reflection. On the other hand, forming irrational opinions is done on the spot—it is convenient for humans to pass instant judgments.

What makes this phenomenon attractive is the tendency of the mind to engage in oversimplification. We see this in the case of a quack doctor who diagnosed all his patients' ailments as either internal or external. To patients with internal problems he prescribed penicillin, and to the ones with external complaints he recommended iodine.

We could miss out on the wonderful world of color—purple, blue, green, yellow, red, orange, and pink—and still see the world only in terms of black and white. For further clarity we need to see different *shades* of the same color, such as royal blue, navy blue, and sky blue.

It is an oversimplification to divide people as good and bad. Even the best of people have shortcomings and the worst of people have some good qualities. All human beings are imperfect. Each person is unique and could be an individual category. It is human for intelligent people to sometimes act stupidly. When people panic, they sometimes act like deer rushing to the nets while chased by a hunter.

A pathway to clear thinking is to avoid the practice of labeling people. It is inconsiderate to ignore the salient features of a person while highlighting a disability or shortcoming. Thus, an artist may be a talented musician like Stevie Wonder, but dismissed by some people as just a blind man.

Intense emotions are a hindrance to clear thinking. A fanatical devotion to one's nationality or ethnic group makes us blind to the merits of other groups. To fully embrace the values of our own group, whether they are right or wrong, is like uncritically accepting the behavior of a parent under any circumstances.

Truth may well lie at the bottom of a well.

Draw distinct patterns of thought

The human mind craves for clarity and coherence to function smoothly. Whatever information fits into these criteria is easily retained even for a long time. On the contrary, the mind does not easily process information that is incoherent and disorderly. Obviously, we should strive to achieve the former. We illustrate this in the following diagrams.

Disorder to order: the mind craves for coherence.

In diagram A, the points are dispersed and disorderly and make little sense. In diagram B, we know instantly that there are nine points. The mind effortlessly grasps this information because there is order and clarity.

Thus, to improve our memory it is important to take information that is disorderly and rearrange it into patterns that are easy to recall.

The mind also easily remembers things when one set of facts is hooked to another set. Some students in the higher grades do not find it easy to remember the formula for calculating simple interest. Here is an easy way to remember: Take the name Peter and cut out the two *e*'s. Without these two letters you are left with PTR. The formula for simple interest is:

$$SI = \frac{PTR}{100}$$

Where P represents the principal, T the time and R the rate.

Thus the simple interest on $2,000 for three years at 5 percent will be equal to 2,000 multiplied by 3 and further multiplied by 5 over 100. The answer is $300.

Feed the mind with substance

When the mind is constantly receiving various amounts of information, it needs to draw a clear distinction between the major and minor points about a person, place, or thing. The former point is known as the substance, and the latter one as the accident. The character, integrity, and values of a person constitute the substance; clothes, hairstyle, and skin color are the accidents. Clear thinking arises when we put more emphasis on the substance than on the accidents. The latter are not to be ignored, but they are of lesser importance than the substance. Muddled thinking arises when the accidents are given greater prominence, when a person is judged by the color of her skin, for instance, and not by the content of her character. Accidents represent a mass of facts as in a telephone directory; though critical, they do not contain a single sublime idea.

S. I. Hayakawa, a distinguished media critic, claims that in modern television, the image may be more important than the substance.

Reading newspapers and watching television interests me to some degree, but they do not stir my soul. To obtain substance, I read the classics. The tragedies of Shakespeare have shaped my mind. Think of imagery in the line from King Lear: "How sharper than a serpent's tooth it is to have a thankless child!" The New Testament in the Bible, the *Dialogues of Plato*, *History of Western Philosophy*, by Bertrand Russell, and *The Profit*, by Kahlil Gibran, are four of the many works I have read that have enriched me immensely.

Improve the power to analyse

The human mind acts like a diamond: the more facets it has, the more brilliantly it shines. Similarly, the more interests the mind displays, the greater the satisfaction it enjoys.

The ability to analyse and synthesize is key to being able to delve deeply into varied interests. To analyse something is to break it down into its different components; to synthesize is to put the pieces together.

At present we shall talk about analysis; subsequently, we shall discuss synthesis.

An important aspect of the mind's analytical power is to observe that, among things, differences are not absolute. They are not one of kind but one of degree. Thus, the distinction between water and ice is one of degree. Even the difference between the human male and female is not absolute. Anatomically, males have female features and vice versa.

We shall call this invaluable feature the Differential Principle. It clearly explains distinctions found in nature and society. As Denis Diderot[85] (1713–1784) wrote, "From fanaticism to barbarism is only one step."

The Differential Principle gives us insights about society. Crime and virtue are manifested in degrees; for example, assault is more serious than trespassing, and befriending twelve people is nobler than being kind to a single individual. We shall discuss the Differential Principle many times throughout this book.

Returning to the topic of analysis, it is vital to observe that justice and injustice also prevail in degrees. Plato explained justice by saying, "give each man his due." Various societies display justice in various ways. Similarly, qualities of skill, versatility, and artistry differ in degree.

A mark of analytical power is to observe that all things are *relative*. Nothing by itself makes sense unless it is compared to something else. Examples of this idea are shown in the following instances:

- The man who did not have shoes stopped crying when he met the man without feet.
- Age forty may be viewed as the old age of youth, but also as the youth of old age.
- An old-fashioned idea is that strength is a man's charm, while charm is a woman's strength.
- Poverty exists in North America, but it pales into insignificance when compared with poverty in other countries.
- It would be wise to remember that, to an ant, a dewdrop is like a flood.

Philosophically speaking, the relative principle was well illustrated by John Locke[86] (1632-1704), the seventeenth-century British thinker. He claimed that things are good or evil only in reference to pleasure or pain. That which we call good is apt to cause pleasure, or diminish pain, and that which we call evil is apt to cause pain.

Analytical power is fruitful in observing social phenomena. It is true of past ages, as well as in our present age, that as some things get better, other things get worse. The designs of the latest automobiles are marvelous, but traffic congestion is getting worse everywhere. The military might of the world's only superpower is awesome, but the goal of building a structure of peace still remains illusive. Adlai Stevenson[87] remarked on this by saying, "Man has made the deserts bloom, but left the lakes to die."

To what extent a society is democratic is also relative. In the strictest sense of the term, a true democracy has never existed and will probably never exist. If we observe the world, we discover that even the best societies have imperfections. Canada is a great nation and has a very heterogeneous society with diverse nationalities living amicably and productively together, while other groups have many problems integrating into the Canadian mosaic.

Embracing the relative principle empowers my mind, and I hope it will do the same for you. I commend this principle to you. Cherish it and it will open for you fresh and exciting perspectives.

Improve the power to synthesize

Fusing ideas delights the mind. It is like listening to an orchestra, where all the instruments work together harmoniously to create an enchanting symphony. The distinct sounds of the diverse instruments can be clearly heard, yet through the genius of the conductor they are beautifully synthesized.

Further examples of synthesizing musical ideas are found in the marriage of two genres to create a third one. The blues was a rudimentary form of music among blacks in America. From blues music came rhythm, and then both were blended to form rock and roll.

Similarly, in the movie industry, documentaries and dramas were each popular in their own right. Nevertheless, the two were combined to produce documentary dramas to create an even more captivating art form. In the same way, romantic comedies were produced to provide a blended form of entertainment that proved to be very appealing to audiences.

Cutting a skeleton key for the mind

We need a key to unlock the complexities of world politics. It could reveal insights into the behavior of nations from an historical point of view as well as provide a clear vision for the current political scene throughout the world. Hopefully, this key would empower our mind with a greater sense of clarity and confidence.

The key could be stated as follows:

Historically, a nation has no permanent friends or enemies; it has only permanent interests that will ultimately prevail against other interests.

The twentieth century provides good examples. Germany and France fought each other in two bitter world wars. Today they are friends because their economic and political interests have intertwined. Both countries are well integrated through the European Union. Similarly, the former Soviet Union and the United States were allies in World War II. Both countries had a common interest in preventing the expansion of Germany to the East and saving Europe from Nazism. The U.S. and Soviet interests began to clash as soon as World War II ended. The Soviet occupation of Eastern Europe and its threatened expansion to the West alarmed the United States and led to the Cold War, which lasted about forty years. Today the former Soviet and

Eastern Bloc nations are closer again to the United States as their common economic interests dictate them to be.

The key could be applied to two other countries in their history over the decades with the United States: Japan is now a friend, while Iran has changed from being an ally to an enemy. This skeleton key indeed provides us with *flashes of wisdom* in politics and history.

III. Training the mind to be vibrant

A custom-made violin produced by a master craftsman is a remarkable musical instrument. As the strings quiver with excitement, a plethora of feelings resonate in the soul. The range includes joy, comfort, and love. The resonance that makes the mind vibrant sets in motion many positive consequences.

Great ideas are conceived through the vibrancy of the human mind. In fact, all ideas originate in the human mind. An ocean liner, a skyscraper, or an opera were all, at one time, only an idea. Later these ideas were developed and became realities. For this reason, many philosophers believe that ideas rule the world and that ideas constitute the ultimate reality.

Powerful thoughts resonate with each other and make the mind vibrant. When hindsight is combined with foresight, it creates insight. This is evident in a game of chess. Experience of past strategies, combined with anticipation of future strategies, gives the player a triumphant outcome.

Like the body, the mind must be exercised and trained in order to become vibrant. When inactive, the body turns sluggish and lacks energy. Restoring the body to physical fitness not only improves the body but also improves the mind, because there is an intimate connection between the two.

For its own sake, the mind also needs to be exercised and stimulated. Otherwise, it functions below par and tends to be lethargic, a condition psychologists call mental inertia.

Thinking exercises the mind. The more we ponder, the easier it becomes. As the body is maintained through regular workouts, the mind must be kept vibrant through regular challenges and daily learning. The principle that living is learning polishes the mind and adds to its vibrancy. A well-honed mind is like a well-toned body. All of us need to be graduates in the school of life.

In our daily lives we must nourish ourselves with mental stimulation, such as attending an interesting lecture, admiring a beautiful painting, or reading an inspiring book. A vibrant mind provides us with *flashes of wisdom and moments of delight*.

Strive to be original

> *All good things which exist are the fruits of originality.*
> *—John Stuart Mill (1806-1873)[88]*

Pablo Picasso (1881–1973)[89] displayed wonderful originality when he took the skeleton of a fish and turned it into a fascinating work of art. The symmetrical shape of the bones set in a blue background was elegant to behold.

Originality consists not only in doing things differently but also in doing them better. I. W. Hitchinson defines originality as a "pair of fresh eyes." It is not difficult to express fresh ideas and opinions; we do so by modifying old ideas and opinions to appear brief and bright. Thus, we become original in our own way.

Changing clichés provides a fine opportunity to appear original. When Mae West was asked how the men in her life were, she replied that she was more concerned about the life in her men. Oscar Wilde took familiar sayings and applied his wit. "Familiarity," he said, "breeds contempt and children." And again, "Nothing succeeds like excess."

As anything has got to come out of something, perish the thought that one can be wholly original. Eminent thinkers and writers have borrowed freely from one another.

In the field of literature, scores of authors have shaped their works on the substance and style of Shakespeare. As Ben Johnson wrote, Shakespeare belonged not to any one age but for all times. Moreover, the Bard was influenced by Virgil, the ancient Roman poet.

In philosophy, Plato and Aristotle are considered the fathers of knowledge, yet Aristotle was profoundly influenced by Plato, and Plato himself acknowledged his debt to Socrates[90] (470–399 BC).

In science, Albert Einstein built his theories on the findings of Isaac Newton, who, in turn, based his ideas on the experiments of Copernicus[91] (1473–1543).

Borrowing ideas came easily to extraordinary minds, and it should come easy for ordinary people. The experience is exhilarating.

Examples of originality that can be emulated are found abundantly in the realm of art. Marc Chagall was famous for creating mobiles. Lovers, flowers, and fish were freed from earthly gravity to take part in an exuberant dance that is lovely to behold. Numerous possibilities exist for anyone to create fascinating mobiles.

It is possible to acquire a touch of genius if we cultivate a superior way of seeing. A child was asked how to overcome gravity while using a pen in space. Instantly, he replied, "Use a pencil."

Picasso said that an ordinary painter depicted the sun as a yellow spot, whereas an extraordinary painter transformed a yellow spot into the sun.

Sharpen your memory

Our memory is our mind's storehouse, a reservoir of accumulated learning. Cicero[92] (106– 43 BC) said that "memory is a treasury and guardian of all thoughts." To a psychologist, memory is an indicator that learning has persisted over time. There is no need to worry if we have memory lapses because it is a common human condition that applies even to the brightest people. The important thing is what measures we take to maintain and improve our memory. Fortunately, proven psychological techniques are available to achieve this. Diligent practice is all that is needed. Here are six techniques.

1. Registration

The first step to acquiring a good memory is to be selective about the thoughts we hold important. We may do so by being very mindful of them amid a clutter of ideas. Our mind goes through a screening process where we give greater priority to some ideas than to others. We all have heard the complaint, "You're not listening to me." Sometimes the complaint is justified because our minds have not registered the words. By being alert and attentive to the speaker, we are more likely to register and thus remember what has been said.

2. Retention

To function well it is crucial to store vital information in our long-term memory. Sometimes we do this by creating a hook to hang this information on, such as an acronym. An acronym is an effective way of remembering a fact or formula. For example, "SCUBA" is an acronym for Self-Contained Underwater Breathing Apparatus. Also, the three *L*'s representing life, love, and laughter can best be retained in our mind as the ingredients for a happy life.

3. Retrieval

Sometimes a fact may be on the tip of our tongue but remain elusive. Retrieving information is a hard part of memory function, but fortunately there are ways to polish our methods of recall.

As our five senses are intimately connected to us, much of the knowledge we gather is deeply imbedded within us. Multisensory perception is a powerful tool for registering, retraining, and retrieving our thoughts and ideas.

Forming mental images jogs our memory. We cannot easily forget the picture when for the first time he gently poured the wine, or she sweetly consented to dance. When mental images are funny, sad, or romantic, they tend to be memorable.

The sound of music also activates our recollection when we still hear the tune in our mind of a waltz we danced to at a wedding ten years ago. The experience is like watching a video with clarity and precision. Another experience that may strike us forcefully is the unique accents of people or their wit and wisdom. We both see and hear them in our mind.

Connecting our experiences with the sense of taste enables our encounter to linger longer. Who could forget the banquet of quail and caviar served with wild rice and tropical fruit? We remember the people and the taste of food that was sweet, spicy, and pungent even though it happened a decade ago.

Our sense of touch also triggers our memory. Excellent mastery in playing the piano produces an amazing feature of how the two hands coordinate in playing the rhythm and the melody. The harmony is made possible by the "fingers doing the thinking" through an instant recollection of the notes.

Another event that may stir our soul is a final kiss or a tender embrace where we felt the warmth of another person. Along with the sense of touch, we may also see and hear the other person as if he or she were actually present.

The smell of grass may remind us of our trek into the countryside every summer, climbing hills and rolling on the grass. The aroma of lavender, rosemary, or thyme may remind us of places that are our own little Shangri-La, a place originally described in the 1933 novel *Lost Horizon*, by British author James Hilton.

Multisensory perception sharpens our memory through the principle of association. In all of the examples cited above, we remember best when one thing is associated with another. Thus, the ideas contained in Rembrandt's[93] (1606–1669) masterpiece *Portrait of an Old Man (The Rabbi)* are eternal. They convey the message about the venerability of old age in every era.

The senses are experienced either individually or in combination. In either case, it is the mind that filters the information, organizes it, and makes sense out of it. Seeing and hearing often act in tandem. Watching a couple dancing the tango, for instance, is pleasing to the eye, and listening to the melody is thrilling to the ear.

4. Stimulation (neurobics)

Dr. Lawrence C. Katz and Manning Rubin presented an exciting new concept called neurobics in their book, *Keeping Your Brain Alive.* Dr. Katz was professor of neurobiology at Duke University Medical Center in North

Carolina. Mr. Rubin also wrote the book *60 Ways to Relieve Stress in 60 Seconds.*

Just as aerobics lead to physical fitness, neurobics bring about mental fitness. The authors present several mental exercises to give the brain a full work out, enabling it to remain young and vibrant. Keeping the brain in shape is important because neuron cells are constantly decaying and dying. Through mental activity it is possible to grow new neurons to offset the loss. This growth takes place even in old age.

Reading, writing, or engaging in challenging tasks like playing chess or doing crossword puzzles activates the brain. One thing that should not be permitted is to allow your brain to atrophy due to lack of stimulation. The best safeguard against atrophy is to always be open to learning. In fact, living is learning.

Mental stimulation is vital for the production of nutrients that grow brain cells to keep the brain nimble and young. The new cells combine with existing cells to create new pathways and circuits. A dense network of connections is woven together to process information in an astonishing manner.

The authors assert that the brain tends to grow in areas where it is used the most. Thus, among cab drivers the brain is most developed in areas where it is devoted to mapping. The same principle is true for scientists, artists, and writers. The authors also offer the comforting message that the power of the mind need not significantly decline in old age. The brain grows additional neurons and forms new connections, fostering mental activity.

Grandparents could have a mind as sharp as their grandchildren, particularly if they cultivate their imagination throughout their lives.

5. Change your routine

Following a dull daily routine does not help to keep the mind sharp and flexible. The mind needs variety, so changing your routine will make it more receptive to new thoughts and ideas. Simple measures like driving or walking on new routes, meeting new people, and forming new interests will help stimulate your mind.

6. Be a thinker, not a drinker

Drinking wine in moderation gives the feeling of relaxation and encourages people to engage in spirited conversation. This fact is well captured in the Latin proverb *In Vino Veritas:* "With wine comes the truth." Excessive alcohol consumption, however, undermines our health, impairs the brain, and clouds our judgment.

A range of wine and spirits are available to suit every pallet. Expand the rich experience of wine tasting to include gin, rum, whiskey, and Kahlua.

Elevate the mind

Oliver Wendell Holmes[94] (1809–1894) wrote, "The human mind, once stretched by a new idea, never regains its original dimensions."[95] Once you touch a hot stove, the memory of the pain still lingers long afterwards.

It is a welcome relief from the humdrum of daily life to occasionally engage in elevated thinking. Such thinking can draw us away from boredom and put us in an exhilarating mood. This mood is an almost perfect condition for the mind to be creative and imaginative.

By looking at life and nature anew, we acquire exciting new perspectives. Though life exists in multiple forms, all life is connected. The basic chemistry of all organisms, from the amoeba to a human, is strikingly similar. The same twenty amino acids occur in all life forms, from bacteria to man. Good reasons exist for us to be humble about our kinship with other forms of life, but an acknowledgement of this humility itself is a mark of wisdom.

Our link with the animal world becomes more evident as we ascend the scale in the animal kingdom. While sharing common features with most mammals, we are very close to the primates. For example, chimpanzees possess 98 percent of the chromosomes found in humans.

Our breadth of vision is widened when we realize that all of humankind shares a common affinity with the entire animal world, particularly the higher forms of life. We must, however, balance our animal heritage with the immense power of our minds, which distinctly sets us apart.

There is one striking feature about the animal world from which we humans could learn a few lessons. Animals in general, like people, are social, but people also fight one another. While animals kill for food and to protect their territory, human beings torture, commit mass murder, and go to war. The social behavior of animals is astonishing. A swarm of honeybees cooperate to produce honey, while a herd of elephants forage together peacefully. Wild dogs work together as a team to bring down a wildebeest, and lions stick together as a pride. Different species of animals congregate in groups to form a common defence against predators. Sheep, deer, and bison find security in numbers and are particularly protective of their young. The attractive qualities of animals prompted Walt Whitman[96] (1819–1892) to write:

> I think I could turn and live with animals,
> They are so placid and self-contained
> I stand and look at them long and long.

While engaging in elevated thinking, we may form a fellowship of heart and mind with those who are like-minded. In this way we may gather *flashes of wisdom and moments of delight.*

Inspire the mind

Like the body, the mind also needs to be nourished. When the mind is inspired by nature, it gives us fresh perspectives on life.

It was left to the genius of Paul Cézanne (1839–1906), the French impressionist painter, to discover an amazing feature of nature. He wrote that all the multitudinous forms and shapes in nature are ultimately rooted in three basic forms: the cone, the cylinder, and the sphere.

The Earth itself is like a sphere, though an imperfect one. It is, however, a beautiful sphere with an immense variety of green and luscious vegetation. It has several million types of plants, but they all have three basic characteristics: the root, the stem, and the flower. The whole of vegetation seems to cry out in unison that, although we are all different, in essence we are the same. The essence of nature is beautiful, simple, and profound. The Brundtland Report[97] echoes this sentiment when it states that although the world is divided, "The Earth is one."

Marcus Aurelius[98] (121–180), the Roman emperor who stands out as a philosopher in a long line of tyrants, had an interesting perspective. "All things come from nature; subside in it and go back to it."

Another aspect of nature that enlivens the mind is to understand that we are made of the same stuff as the universe. The constituent elements of our bodies, the Earth, moon, and stars are more or less the same, though in different proportions. An examination of moon rocks and meteorites reveals that the chemical compositions are similar to that of Earth.

The periodic table indicates that there are 103 elements on Earth. Current observations suggest that the same elements that exist on Earth are found in the universe, though in different proportions. Thus, the Earth and its inhabitants are very much a part of the universe. These scientific facts should inspire our minds to realize that, while dwelling as we do in our tiny niche, we can still, to some degree, comprehend the composition and vastness of the universe.

Expand the mind through culture

> *Men's natures are alike;*
> *it is their cultures that carry them far apart.*
> —*Confucius*

Culture is a way of life. It is only within the milieu of culture that the mind can flower. Individual excellence is often the product of cultural expression. The achievements of popular and classical artists are inseparable from their cultures.

Culture at its best makes us feel inclusive and broad-minded. Under a liberal attitude, the mind sparkles when we marry our own cultural preferences with other cultural choices. Thus, while we enjoy our own genre in music, we expand our horizons when we taste other musical genres. When we are excited about the strategy in our own favorite sport, we may also appreciate the strategies of other sports.

The mind, according to its true nature, is expansive. It thirsts not only for deep knowledge but also for breadth. In the area of culture, it excels when it fuses together a number of art forms or divergent ideas. Our minds are likely to be enriched when we simultaneously combine the enjoyment of Chinese ballet with rock and roll, for instance, or synthesize primitive art with modern art.

Pablo Picasso was a genius who provided real intellectual pleasure by making modern art produce an elegant imprint of primitive art—the old became new again. Primitive art was truly original when it attempted to capture the spirit of an animal by elegantly depicting it viscerally. Picasso borrowed this idea from primitive art, yet he was original when he created his own art form. In a single portrait, he often represented a multidimensional view of a person, an animal, or a thing. He was able to achieve a feat that even an ordinary camera was unable to do.

The intermingling of primitive art with modern art has captured the imagination of art lovers the world over. It is an example of how the interaction of two or more cultural art forms stirs the human mind.

If our mind is to sparkle, we must be daring. After accepting all that is best in our culture, we must boldly reject whatever is absurd. In the early 1970s, a television advertisement in the U.S. promoted the idea of "country freshness" from smoking a certain type of cigarette (Salem). Many people recognized the falsehood of this concept and cigarette advertising was sooned banned from American airwaves. Now smoking bans abound in cities throughout the world Thanks to initiatives like these, the lives of millions of people have been saved.

While culture broadens the mind, it can also narrow the mind. If people unquestionably accept the extreme positions of their subculture, the capacity of their mind to think clearly is undermined.

An example of this is when certain tribes worship snakes and eat rodents because those are customs in their culture. Though those examples are extreme, but there are still situations in which people find it difficult to think independently of their culture. Very often, their way of thinking is a reflection of the ideas and values of their culture.

Culture is like an invisible garment woven around us from our earliest years; it is made of the way we eat, the way we walk, the way we greet people. Some social scientists have argued that many people are like puppets dancing to the tune of their culture. Often this behavior is healthy, such as when we value human dignity and the sanctity of human life. At other times people are cruel and inhuman, like when they blindly follow the dictates of their subculture. The mass killings committed by suicide bombers are partly explained in terms of their subculture, which supports their violent behavior.

Form a hybrid of ideas

For the mind to dazzle, it needs to be well nourished by a broad range of interests. It is the cross-fertilization of ideas that creates a new hybrid of ideas that are rich and refreshing.

The cultural riches of the world offer the mind exciting new perspectives. As Alexander Pope[99] (1688–1744) wrote, "Let your mind with extended view, survey mankind from China to Peru."[100]

Let's distil some folksy proverbs of wit and wisdom. These proverbs can be interpreted in more than one way. I suggest one approach (presented in *italics*), but you are invited to interpret them differently. It should be noted that it is difficult to explain eloquent proverbs in equally eloquent language.

Do not call a crocodile big mouth, until you have crossed the river.
When a person is powerful, bide your time before you criticize him.
A lizard on a cushion will still seek a leaf.
A natural instinct will prevail even over a luxury.

Man is made of marble and mud.[101]
Man has both noble and ignoble qualities.

An arch never sleeps.[102]
People who bear heavy burdens are not at ease.

Much bending breaks the body. Much unbending breaks the mind.
An inflexible attitude causes mental turmoil.

Fire makes mud hard but melts gold.

Suffering makes hard-hearted people even more hard-hearted and sensitive people even more sensitive.

Wolves fear the fog.
Exposure to light is an obstacle to stealth.

When wood breaks, it can be repaired, but ivory breaks forever.
Selfish attitudes can be corrected, but a broken heart remains broken.

We shall obtain a deeper delight when we interpret these proverbs metaphorically.

While a person should be proud of his national culture, his mind's interest cannot be limited to national confines because the mind's power is not limited. As previously discussed, to be exclusively devoted to one's culture is shortsighted, and anything in excess is ugly. Militant behavior arises when people believe that their own culture, country, or creed is superior to that of others. This is ethnocentrism, a catalyst for wars that cause much bloodshed.

For true nobility of thought, our mind must transcend national boundaries. We can find goodness and excellence aplenty in the world. Some eminent thinkers who displayed this type of spirit were Albert Schweitzer (1875–1965)[103], Ludwig Van Beethoven (1770–1827), and Marie Curie[104] (1867–1934). They were more akin to humanity at large than to their own countries.

Ibn Khaldun[105] (1332–1406), an Arab thinker in the fourteenth century, coined the term civilization. He conceived the concept in the singular, as a human enterprise global in scope. In his view, "The history of mankind is a movement from ignorance to knowledge, and knowledge in all its aspects is a common resource of humanity."[106]

Draw on the unconscious

Tell me in one word, said the king, what is the essence of wisdom? The sage pondered for a while and mentioned the word *carrots*. The king was baffled. He demanded an explanation. "Carrots," said the sage, "remind us that the best part of a thing may lie hidden and buried. Discovering it is hard work."

What is unseen may be more important than what is seen. It is the unseen root that must be watered to sweeten the fruit. It is the unseen sap that nourishes the tree. It is the hidden seed that possesses an innate power to grow into a mighty tree.

Leading thinkers have claimed that like the seed, the human mind is endowed with a hidden power. We may not be conscious of this power, but it does influence our motivation and behavior profoundly.

Sigmund Freud[107] (1856–1939) believed that a part of the mind is like an iceberg submerged below the surface and moved by underlying currents.

To better understand the mind, we must understand the unconscious. In our daily life the unconscious process may affect us in diverse ways. For example, a person may not look forward to his dental appointment because he fears a painful extraction. Subsequently, when he forgets to keep his appointment, the reason might not lie in his poor memory, but in his unconscious wish to escape from an ordeal.

It is common for people to forget the loans they have borrowed but not the loans they have granted. Perhaps it is their unconscious instinct for financial advantage that prompts them to forget what they borrowed and to remember what they have lent.

The behavior of people is, to a significant degree, determined by factors about which they are not quite aware. The unconscious processes of the mind may therefore be identified as those thoughts, wishes, and fears about which a person is unaware but which still influence him significantly. He may have experienced certain ideas and feelings, but he cannot directly bring them back to awareness. Sometimes the reality we refuse to face may get buried in our unconscious mind.

According to Carl Jung, the way some people fall in love offers us interesting clues about the power of the unconscious. When attracted to a person of the opposite sex, some people are unable to exercise rational control over their thoughts. They seem to be acting on the orders of a powerful force within them. For a man this force is the "woman" hidden within him, which Jung referred to as the anima. A woman, too, may have a man hidden within her, which Jung referred to as the animus.

The anima and the animus are idealized images of the opposite sex that men and women have formed since their early childhood. These images could be composite characters and are of a vague nature. In the words of Jung, "It is the presence of the anima that causes a man to fall suddenly in love when he sees a woman for the first time and knows at once that this is 'the one.'"[108] In this situation, the man feels as if he has known this woman intimately for a long time, but to an outsider it looks like odd behavior.

Similarly, a woman falls for a man led by the animus within her. Her father or other men may have influenced her animus. The animus might personify the attractive qualities of male behavior, such as courage, enterprise, wit, and a spirit of adventure.

Jung did not discuss the attraction that people have for members of the same sex. His analysis is therefore limited because homosexual behavior did not matter in his theories.

The unconscious need not be feared. If we boldly recognize it and accept it, the unconscious becomes a guide and a friend. To appreciate its importance, we must realize that the conscious mind is only a part of man's total mind. As long as man functions only on the ordinary level of the conscious mind he is not using his full mental potential.

By integrating the unconscious with the conscious, one can sharpen the imagination and achieve mental harmony. Many painters, musicians, philosophers, and scientists owe some of their best ideas to inspiration that appears suddenly from the realm of the unconscious. While one draws upon the resources of the conscious mind to engage in logical analysis, one needs to fall back upon the unconscious mind in order to be enriched by intuition and inspiration.

To be conscious of the unconscious is to discover the hidden treasures that lie within our own depths, as in the depths of most things.

Behold the stars

An interest in the heavenly bodies lifts us out of boredom. A heavenly perspective helps us to think more sublimely and feel more nobly when confronted with earthly problems.

Stars played an important role in the lives of primitive people. About 2000 BC, the ancient people of Britain built Stonehenge, which has recently been interpreted as an astronomical observatory. They assembled enormous blocks of stones into an intricate structure from which they could measure the seasons and predict the eclipses of the sun and the moon.

Since early times people have identified the sun's affinity to Earth. Today we know that the sun is composed of about 20 percent helium and 80 percent hydrogen, which is a common element on Earth. The sun is, however, a nuclear furnace with a temperature of fifteen million degrees Celsius. It is constantly emitting a tremendous amount of energy by converting its hydrogen atoms into helium.

We also know that the sun is a star, though it is a modest star when compared with the billions of stars in the universe. By drawing an astrophysical link with the sun, Earth is also able to draw a link with the whole universe.

Richness of understanding is often obtained by looking at things from different angles. The great thing about astronomy is the opportunity it offers the mind to gather many perspectives. When the mind traverses the vast spaces of the universe, it is like an ant crawling from Vancouver to Halifax.

Distances within the universe are so vast that scientists have devised the concept of the light year to measure the distances in space. We know that light travels at a speed of 300,000 kilometers per second, and a light year represents the distance traveled by light during one year.

In the universal scheme of things, Earth appears to play an infinitesimally insignificant role. It is like a drop of water vapor within a large cloud when compared to the stars and galaxies of the universe. Yet, Earth may be the most important part of the universe because it contains life, particularly intelligent human life. Scientists have not ruled out the possibility of tracing primitive forms of life on Mars and of discovering intelligent life in the rest of the universe, but so far they have had no success.

Though man is able to dominate Earth, in astronomical terms he has reason to be humble. His conquests on Earth pale into insignificance when we consider the fact that Earth occupies such a tiny corner within the universe. Yet, he also has good reason to be proud of himself. From his little bluish planet, he has been able through the power of his intellect to understand so much about the heavenly bodies. The heavenly bodies, however, have not been able to understand anything about man. Therein lies man's greatness.

The universe is wonderful, but still more wonderful is the brilliance of man's mind. The wonders of the universe would mean nothing but for the extraordinary ability of man's mind to comprehend these wonders. Through much painstaking effort, man has unravelled some of the mysteries of the universe. We know that though the stars appear haphazard in the night sky, they are nevertheless grouped together in clusters called galaxies. We also know that stars, like people, can be classified as young, middle-aged, and old. Many stars have been identified in age from half a billion years to sixty-five billion years. Within our own times, new stars are born and old stars are dying out.

In the humdrum of life, an interest in the heavens can boost our energy. We may look at the night sky and say in the words of a small child,

> *Twinkle, twinkle little star.*
> *How I wonder what you are.*
> *Up above the world so high,*
> *Like a diamond in the sky.*

Sometimes it is refreshing to be able to look at things with the enthusiasm of a child.

Paradoxes to ponder

What is harder than rock or softer than water? Yet soft water hollows out hard rock. Persevere.
—Ovid[109]

The only certainty is that nothing is certain.

You have to study a great deal to know a little.
—Montesquieu

To know that you do not know is wisdom.
—Lao-tzu[110]

People have one thing in common: they are all different[111]
-- Robert Zend

When people are least sure they are most dogmatic
-- John Kenneth

We learn from experience that men never learn anything from experience[112]
-- George Bernard Shaw

O, what a heaven is love ! O, what a hell ![113]
--Thomas Middleton

60. A Czech-born German writer, Kafka's writings stand unique in Western literature. His most famous work was called "The Metamorphosis."

61. A French sculptor, Rodin was one of the preeminent sculptors of the modern era.

62. Rilke is generally considered the German language's greatest twentieth-century poet.

63. An American visionary, designer, architect, poet, author, and inventor.

64. This preeminent American architect was born in 1929. His buildings, including his private residence, have become tourist attractions. Many museums, companies, and cities seek Gehry's services as a badge of distinction, beyond the product he delivers.

65. Samuel Taylor Coleridge, *The Complete Works of Samuel Taylor Coleridge: With an Introductory Essay* (Harper & brothers, 1856), 130.

66. An English philosopher, essayist, politician, and courtier who is best known for leading the scientific revolution with his "observation and experimentation" theory, which is the way science has been conducted ever since. Francis Bacon, *The Essays Of Francis Bacon* (Houghton, Mifflin, 1908), 159.

67. A German mystic, monk, and writer.

68. An American essayist, social critic, and writer. Henry David Thoreau, *The Writings of Henry David Thoreau* (Houghton, Mifflin, 1937), 249.

69. William James, *The Principles of Psychology* (Courier Dover Publications), 369.

70. An American psychologist and philosopher.

71. Job 28:18, KJV

72. An English poet best-known for his epic poem "Paradise Lost."

73. A Scottish historian, biographer, critic, and essayist. Thomas Carlyle, *The Works of Thomas Carlyle* (C. Scribner's Sons, 1899), 466.

74. A classical Greek writer, 480–406 BC.

75. An Anglo-American poet, regarded by many as the one of the greatest writers of the twentieth century.

76. His best-known work is *Leviathan*, which has had a great impact among writers. David Van Mill, *Liberty, Rationality, and Agency in Hobbes's Leviathan* (SUNY Press,2001), 122.

77. Homer was truly a mysterious poet of epic proportion. There is a myriad of mysteries and discrepancies concerning the history of poet. He is supposedly the author of the *Iliad* and *Odyssey*, two of the most famous works in classical Greek literature.

78. Francis Bacon, *The Essays Of Francis Bacon* (Houghton, Mifflin, 1908).

79. An English poet who lived from 1795 to 1821. His works were noteworthy for their elaborate word choice and sensual imagery. John Keats, *The Finer Tone: Keats' Major Poems* (Johns Hopkins Press, 1953), 60.

80. A German idealist philosopher.

81. A Swiss psychiatrist and founder of analytical psychology, a school of thought whose aim is the personal experience of the deep forces and motivations

underlying human behavior. Carl Gustav Jung, *Man and His Symbols* (Aldus Books in association with W. H. Allen 1964).

82. Originally, this concept was advanced by Alfred Adler (see "Aiming for achievement" in Chapter 5).

83. William Somerset Maugham, *Collected Plays* (Heinemann, 1952), 291. Maugham was an English playwright, novelist, and short story writer. He was one of the most popular authors of his era, achieving recognition as the highest paid of his profession during the 1930s.

84. An influential English writer of the early twentieth century. His prolific and diverse output included journalism, poetry, biography, Christian apologetics, fantasy, and detective fiction.

85. A French philosopher and writer.

86. Locke argued a government could be legitimate only if it received the consent of the governed through a social contract and protected the natural rights of life, liberty, and property.

87. The American Democratic presidential candidate in 1952 and 1956, who lost both times to Dwight Eisenhower. Adlai Ewing Stevenson, *Speeches* (Random House, 1952), 97.

88. Mill was best known for advocating utilitarianism, the idea that the moral value of an action is determined solely by its contribution to overall usefulness. John Stuart Mill, *On Liberty* (Ticknor and Fields, 1863), 73.

89. A Spanish painter who is best known as the cofounder of Cubism.

90. He is widely credited for laying the foundation of Western philosophy

91. The astronomer who formulated the first modern heliocentric theory of the solar system.

92. He was an orator, statesman, political theorist, lawyer, and philosopher of ancient Rome.

93. Rembrandt is generally considered one of the greatest painters and printmakers in European art history and the most important in Dutch history. American art historian and Rembrandt Biographer John C. Van Dyke commends that, "Rembrandt's domestic troubles served only to heighten and deepened his art, and perhaps his best canvases were painted under stress of circumstances and in sadness of heart. His life is another proof, if heeded, that the greatest truths and beauties are to be seen only through tears.".

94. A physician by profession, Holmes achieved fame as a writer. He was one of the best-regarded American poets of the nineteenth century.

95. Andrew McWilliam, *Percy Longmuir* (J.B. Lippincott Company, 1907), p.333.

96. An American poet, essayist, journalist, and humanist. Walt Whitman, *Walt Whitman* (Sterling Publishing Company, Inc., 1997), 22

97. The 1987 Brundtland Report, titled "Our Common Future," alerted the world to the urgency of making progress toward economic development that could be sustained without depleting natural resources or harming the

environment. Gregory G. Lebel, *Gro Harlem Brundtland, Development., Hal Kane, Our Common Future* (Oxford University Press, 1987), 27

98. He was emperor from 161 until his death. He was the last of the "Five Good Emperors," who governed the Roman Empire from 96 to 180, and is also considered one of the most important Stoic philosophers.

99. He was an English poet and satirist.

100. John Holmes Agnew, Eliakim Littell, *The Eclectic Museum of Foreign Literature, Science and Art* (E. Littell, 1843), p.189.

101. Nathaniel Hawthorne, *The House of Seven Gables*, 1851.

102. James Fergusson, *History of Indian and Eastern Architecture*, 1891.

103. Schweitzer was a versatile genius, excelling as a musician, philosopher, theologian, and physician. He was awarded the Nobel Peace Prize in 1953 recognition of his "Reverence for Life" concept.

104. A Polish-French physicist and chemist, Curie was a pioneer in radioactivity, the first two-time Nobel laureate (the only one in two different sciences), and the first female professor at the Sorbonne.

105. He was a famous historian born in present-day Tunisia.

106. Henry C. Clark, *Compass of Society: Commerce And Absolutism In Old-Regime France* (Lexington Books, 2006), 224.

107. Freud was an Austrian neurologist and the cofounder of the psychoanalytic school of psychology. He is best known for his theories of the unconscious mind, especially involving the mechanism of repression and his redefinition of sexual desire.

108. Carl Gustav Jung, *Man and His Symbols* (Aldus Books in association with W. H. Allen 1964).

109. Ovid (43 BC–AD 17), a Roman poet, wrote on topics of love, abandoned women, and mythological transformations. Kappa Delta Pi (Honor Society), *The Educational Forum* (Kappa Delta Pim 1936), p. 487.

110. Recognized as the fonder of Taoism.

111. Robert Zend, *Beyond Labels* (Hounslow Press, 1982), p.60.

112. Stephen Winsten, *The Quintessence of G.B.S.: The Wit and Wisdom of Bernard Shaw* (Hutchinson, 1949), p.400.

113 Thomas Middleton, The Works of Thomas Middleton (J.C. Nimno, 1885), p.15.

Chapter 3
The Joys of Genuine Intimacy

Chapter 3
The Joys of Genuine Intimacy

The first condition of human goodness is someone to love.
—George Eliot (1818—1860)[114]

George Eliot was a female writer who assumed a male pseudonym in order to be recognized more seriously. Her novels are unique for combining gentle humor with a serious tone. She was one of England's most outstanding novelists of the nineteenth century, portraying English rural life with wit and compassion.

In the Sanskrit language there are ninety-six words for love. Each one denotes a different aspect ranging from love that is tepid to that which is intense, from erotic to romantic. Other languages, too, have a variety of expressions because love is perhaps the strongest of the passions, affecting simultaneously the head, the heart, and senses.

Love in its pure form exists when two people find pleasure in promoting each other's happiness. They strive for mutual benefits by displaying mutual care and concern. John Milton refers to this type of love as the "crown of all bliss."

Love is the salt of life. Just as the finest dishes are flavorless without salt, the finer things of life appear insipid without love. Life is often harsh, but love frees us from its weight and pain. Although life is short, love adds quality by satisfying a deep hunger within us to love and to be loved. A supreme happiness is the conviction that we are loved. When two people share deep feelings of closeness, there exists between them a spirit of *genuine intimacy*. Under this spirit they share with each other a part of themselves. Familiar acts become beautiful, and they may say to each other in the words of Conrad Aiken[115] (1889–1973), "The bread I ate with you was more than bread and the wine I drank with you was more than wine."[116]

With genuine intimacy, your lover becomes a soul mate, an intimate companion for all seasons. Such a lover will be a friend who will come in when the whole world has gone out and will be a friend with whom you can be yourself, adding joy to your life while sharing your grief. There are many dimensions to genuine intimacy. And here we shall discuss them under seven categories. The divisions are somewhat arbitrary because the intertwined categories reflect the manifold aspects of our personality. The seven intimacies are emotional, physical, intellectual, communicative, aesthetic, crisis, and conflict.

I. Emotional intimacy

Becoming lovely in each other's eyes

> *"A loving heart is the truest wisdom."*[117]—
> *Charles Dickens (1812–1870)*[118]

One of the sweetest of all sounds is praise. Humans crave appreciation. This urge is best satisfied through emotional intimacy, which is sweet to experience because two people become lovely in each other's eyes for their numerous acts of kindness. Together, they become more energized and fruitful as they view life afresh. Their love for each other is not blind but bound. This is important because in today's faceless world, love cushions us against anxiety, which is the common lot of all mankind. Even during the best of times, dealing with life alone is often weary. But with the mutual support of a loving companion, burdens appear light, challenges are exciting, the impossible seems possible, and the far appears as near.

Adults, no less than children, yearn for love. Just as the eye needs light and the ear needs music, the heart craves for love. We all want to be wanted and confirmed. A hunger exists among people for genuine intimacy, and when this hunger is satisfied, we feel complete; when unsatisfied, we feel incomplete.

Evening offers a wonderful chance for pleasant conversations, preceded by a hearty supper and a glass of wine. A good night's sleep and a fine morning may sparkle your day, and nothing is more important than this day. A day itself is a part of life.

The spark of love in genuine intimacy is like a fire, which must be stoked to be kept alive. Otherwise, it will flicker away. Sometimes the brightness within us goes out, but it can be relit into a flame by our partner. We owe it to our partner to rekindle that light.

Graham Greene[119] (1904–1991) offered a note of caution about intimacy, however. He claimed that, "No human being truly understands another, and no one can arrange another's happiness." The closest we come to this ideal is through genuine intimacy.

Add more romance to life

Perish the thought that only young people are romantic. One can be so at any age because the heart that loves is always young. I witnessed an expression of romantic love at a dance for seniors. A gallant couple were honored for their diamond-wedding anniversary. The man was eighty-two years old and the woman was eighty. Their love for each other was evident in the sparkle in their eyes. He wore a rose in his lapel that made him look young. She looked youthful, perhaps because she felt youthful. While they danced in rhythmic union, their feelings for each other seemed to be running in their veins. The music captured their sentiments when it echoed through the dance hall.

> He remembered the first time he met her,
> He remembered the first thing she said.
> He remembered the fun and the teasing,
> And the night that she came to his bed.
> He remembered her sweet way of singing,
> "Honey, has something gone wrong?"
> He remembered the fun and the teasing,
> and the reason he wrote her this song.
> I'll give you a daisy a day, dear.
> I'll give you a daisy a day.
> I'll love you until the rivers run still
> and the four winds we know blow away.[120]

The music and the dance touched the audience. There were many whose eyes were moist. A couple is swept by romantic love when they get something from each other that they cannot get from any other person. As Elizabeth Ashley[121] wrote, "In a great romance, each person plays a part that the other person really likes." We must realize, of course, that in a relationship we cannot expect our mate to fulfil all our needs. No one person can be everything to someone else. What is most rewarding is for partners to live for each other. We shall see in the next section that unrealistic expectations are a threat to emotional intimacy. One way to intensify a romance is to satisfy our urge for belonging while at the same time maintaining our separateness. These opposite feelings express one aspect of the many contradictions inherent in human nature. Belonging means being together, but no person can own another. Through separation, the absence provokes an invisible "presence."

The charms of platonic love

Young Plato and his friends, Glaucon and Ariston, had a drinking party by night to discuss the deeper meaning of love and intimacy. In Greek, this dialogue was called a symposium. What transpired at this session was some of the most beautiful passages on this subject ever recorded in literature.

A sense of belonging, according to Plato, is deeply rooted in human nature. Any man or woman left to himself or herself alone is in some respects inadequate and insufficient. The individual constitutes only a "half" and needs to become a "whole." Falling in love is a powerful craving for a person whom you consider to be your "other half." It is only in union with your "other half" that you become a "whole," or still better, be a wholesome personality. Plato claimed that two people become really "complete" when they are in union, intellectually, emotionally, and physically. These unions follow each other naturally just as night follows day.

The three types of relationships are enriching because they intertwine and complement each other. When a man and a woman are thus united, they become two in one and the woman, said Plato, is the "better half," a term that has survived to this day. Clearly, Plato was a friend of women. When intellectual and emotional intimacies are powerful, physical attraction may creep in, and this is natural. Harriet Taylor, a married woman, had a great intellectual relationship with John Stuart Mill, the English philosopher. She collaborated with him for over a decade and eventually married him upon the death of her husband. Could a man and a woman engage in deep intellectual and emotional intimacies without any physical relationship? Plato says that this is possible, but it is not for everybody. Strangely, the modern interpretation of the "platonic relationship" is quite different from Plato's ideas on male-female relationships.

A three-fold union between two people could be between members of the same sex. Plato was thus the first great champion of homosexual and lesbian rights. He, however, expressed some reservation when this idea clashed with his advocacy of unions between bright men and women to bring forth bright children. The platonic idea of sharing and belonging is eloquently expressed by Percy Bysshe Shelley in "Love's Philosophy":

> Nothing in the world is single;
> All things by a law divine
> In one spirit meet and mingle.
> Why not I with thine?
>
> See, the mountain kiss high heaven,
> And the waves clasp one another;
> No sister flower could be forgiven
> If it distained its brother;
> And the sunlight clasp the earth,
> And the moonbeams kiss the sea;
> And what are all these kisses worth,

If thou kiss not me?

The lofty ideas of Plato and Shelley about two people complementing each other also seem to be based on a scientific principle. Niels Bohr,[122] the famous physicist, expounded the principle of complementarity as a universal principle. He claimed that there are always two sides or parts to everything that is a whole in the universe. Thus, a piece of wood is both matter and energy, and a beam of light is both a wave and a particle.

Keep excitement alive

An obstacle to sustaining a romance is boredom. Through familiarity, partners may tire of each other over time. This is minimized by viewing one's partner in exciting new ways. Sexually speaking, the most important part of the body is the brain. Sexual attraction and intense passion are emotions stirred by the brain. It is only our thinking that makes the model more attractive than the maid, the actor more than the waiter.

Through the imagination of role-playing, it is possible to turn our partner into whatever person we desire, provided it is mutually acceptable. The partner may become in our eyes a prince or a princess, a paramour or a mistress, a friend, a spouse, or even an idol. Excitement is further nourished, as we shall see later, through communication, aesthetic, crisis, and even conflict intimacies.

Add pizzazz to life as a protection against boredom and monotony. The joint appreciation of nature, music, and art has a therapeutic effect on the soul. Walk together under the western sky on a summer evening, sip tea, and watch the sun go down.

Eyes: – a gateway to the heart

William Hazlitt[123] (1778–1830) wrote, "You can see the force of human genius in the works of William Shakespeare." In Shakespeare's *Merchant of Venice*, Antonio asked Bassanio how he could fall in love with Portia without having conversed with her. Bassanio replied in these immortal words, "But from her eyes, I did receive speechless messages of love." Portia's smile of love was enchanting. Through her eye contact, she perhaps made a seductive advance to Bassanio that swept him off his feet. Eyes are a gateway to the inner being of a person, and their messages are very revealing. In Indian movies, where explicit love scenes are discouraged, beautiful actresses convey their feelings of passionate love through a range of eye movements. Sidonie-Gabrielle Colette[124] (1873–1954) conveyed a sensuous idea in this passage: "When she raised her eyelids, it is as if she were taking off her clothes."

It would be exciting for partners to communicate through their eyes alone. Intense feelings of affection, gratitude, joy, passion, romance, tenderness, and sexual desire are all communicated through the eyes. A loving gaze may capture for the partners their innermost feelings.

Present pleasant surprises

We soon tire of routine. It is essential, at least occasionally, to do unexpected things that are pleasing, such as:

- Send a birthday gift marked "ESPN" with an explanatory note stating, "Exciting Sex Promised Nightly."
- Pause at the porch, ring the doorbell, and greet her with a kiss, a rose, and a bottle of champagne.
- Use your reddest lipstick and mail him a love song, "Sealed with a Kiss."
- Mail a bottle of chili sauce with a note, "I like it hot."
- Go on a canoe ride at midnight under the full moon. The late Pierre Berton[125] (1920–2004) defined a Canadian as, "Someone who can make love in a canoe."[126]
- Mix your own custom-made drink and name it after your lover, such as, "Stephen's Sling" or "Gail's Grand Marnier Nightcap."
- Have your partner's portrait painted from a photograph.
- Present your woman with colorful lingerie or your man with silk shorts.
- Know your partner's music taste and create a custom CD of romantic love songs.
- Be your partner's one-person fan club. Cheer your partner's achievements.
- Name your new boat, should you have one, after your partner.
- Write love letters to your partner, particularly when you are apart.[127]

There is no limit to the ingenuity of partners to come up with ideas to break monotony and add spice to life.

A sense of belonging is heightened by periods of separation. Samuel Johnson[128] (1709–1784) wrote that even the "the most tender love requires renewal by intervals of absence." We cannot spend every waking hour with our partner. We must be prepared to move aside from time to time and let our partner be free, like a butterfly. We should drink the same wine but from different cups, eat the same food but from different plates. We should occasionally stand apart from each other like the pine and the oak, savor the same song but sing different parts. Hold your partner tightly but do not smother, cling to your partner but allow spaces between you. Grow mutually, but also individually.

A sense of belonging and separation are well balanced when each of the partners engages in self-discovery, a process of trying to better understand oneself. What is it you really stand for? What are your dreams and what is it you really want out of life? Answering these questions will enhance your romantic life. Together you will sing in sunshine and rain but will also have a chance to be in solitude and enjoy its silence. You'll ride the same canoe but use two paddles.

Impediments to intimacy

Socrates was a serious man, but in this statement he was humorous. He urged all men to marry. "If you get a good wife," he said, "you will become very happy; if you get a bad one, you will become a philosopher, and that is good for every man."

We would do well to be aware of the impediments to love. Though it is natural to love, this urge may be thwarted by negative life experiences commencing in early childhood. A child who has not experienced the tender feelings of love carries the risk of growing into an adult who finds it difficult to sustain a healthy, intimate relationship. What is more likely, however, is for a child who has been inadequately loved to become an adult with an inadequate capacity to love and be loved. These adults could be good parents, intelligent and reasonable people in many respects, but in the long run, they shy away from engaging in happy, intimate relationships. Here again we emphasize the Differential Principle, how people display diverse degrees of intimacy in their marital or romantic relationships. A primary cause for the breakup of unions is the inability on the part of one or both partners to be intimate. In spite of these barriers, emotional intimacy can be cultivated and nourished to bloom into an exciting relationship.

II. Physical intimacy

Lions mate at all seasons and so do human beings, but our mating behavior is not merely physical—it could be spiritual, or even sublime.

The best gift one can offer another is oneself. There are few things finer in this world than the expression of one's most tender feelings.

Physical union is a form of communication where the partners give to each other something that is a part of them. It does not consist of a single act but of several acts forming a single drama. It is delightful when it is sustained over a period of time, intertwined with love, affection, and tenderness. "High quality sex," said Alex Comfort[129] (1920-2000), "only comes with love." An act of kindness, a word of praise, or a romantic attitude heightens sexual pleasure. When love swells there is something more than a passionate interest in another body. There now exists a passionate interest in another person.

While physical attraction is a major factor in physical intimacy, there's something more important. As Ralph Waldo Emerson wrote, "Any extraordinary degree of beauty in man or woman involves a moral charm."

An amorous appetizer

Considerable scientific evidence exists to prove the beneficial effects of touching. Nurses are trained in therapeutic touch to alleviate pain and bring comfort to patients. Observation shows that the power of touch triggers important physiological changes. The most significant change is the healing effect, but other changes include the easing of tensions and freeing a person of minor depression and anxiety.

The loving touch of partners works miracles. Foremost among the benefits of touching is that it reinforces a sense of belonging, a deep human desire. Hugging, combined with pleasant conversation, provides intimate companionship, a beautiful complement to intellectual and emotional intimacies. A loving touch builds self-esteem and thereby helps to dispel loneliness and overcome fears. In a word, it has a therapeutic effect. A morning hug can make you feel good all day. Kathleen Keating, in *The Hug Therapy Book*, states that hugging delays the aging process. While everyone might not agree with this claim, it is clear that hugging is beneficial to people of all ages.

Kisses: the language of love

Kissing is the expression of a passionate urge. With such an urge, both partners convey through their lips and tongues intense feelings of love and tenderness. The feelings come from their hearts and return to their hearts. Kissing is an intimate act in which the partners feel each other's breath. Breath is the essence of life because it sustains our existence. The oxygen we breathe is circulated throughout the body, particularly to the brain, enabling it to think and feel.

When partners share their breath they offer each other a most sacred treasure. "A passionate kiss," writes Barbara DeAngelis[130], "stands alone, even above intercourse as an act in which both lovers are equally open to one another. Each offers the other that which is sacred, each receives the sacrament back. We may think that we are just smooching, but in truth, our souls are breathing together." A passionate kiss is perhaps the ultimate form of oral satisfaction. DeAngelis further suggests that the mouth is the doorway to your partner's inner being. In this way, "the act of kissing imitates the act of sexual intercourse. A part of you enters your partner's body and a part of you receives his or her body into yours."

Kisses are indeed the language of love. They express myriad feelings even more meaningfully than words. A pledge, a promise, and a commitment of love are concluded when sealed with a kiss.

Enjoy the prelude to sex

Appetizers are a good prelude to fine dining. A variety of odors mixed with pleasant conversation makes a dinner memorable. According to an old adage, to make love in the evening, start in the morning. The prelude to coitus heightens the pleasure of sexual intercourse. The skillful lover knows the adventure of exploring and finding the erogenous zones of the body. They are like natural springs that lie hidden beneath the surface. An ecstatic delight arises when lovers probe deeper and deeper into the sources of these springs. When they succeed in opening them, there gushes forth a torrent of love and excitement.

The lips and hands are natural tools for awakening the erogenous zones of the lovers' bodies. We saw earlier that kisses constitute the language of love. We shall now find that the hands of both men and women have a magical quality. They convey loving thoughts and feelings even better than words.

"Whatever is in your heart will come out in your hands," one sex therapist has noted. A sensual massage is a delightful experience before, during, and after coitus. While kissing passionately, the partners may gently massage each other's necks and then extend their fingers down the backs, sending shivers of soothing delight.

Let the body become the harp of the soul

Love makes sex better; sex makes love better.

The harp can be viewed as a mere physical device but also as an instrument to produce heavenly music. In lovemaking, the body becomes like a harp to be played artfully, at times slow and at times fast, with caresses, kisses, embraces, and thrust to draw a pair to ecstasy.

Let your sexual union be more than the tingling of bare skin. Let your body become the harp of your soul. Gently tend your lover's body like a harp to produce a soothing music, to ease your ills away. With the tingling of bare skins, make her cry, make her tremble; make her shudder like a dove. Make him sigh, make him shiver, and give him lots and lots of love.

It is through a union of bodies that a pair attains a union of souls. This intimacy is perhaps the deepest and truest expression of love that one can ever experience.   Juliet[131], in a state of orgasmic delight, cries unto Romeo, "My bounty is boundless as the sea, my love as deep, the more I give to thee, the more I have for my love is infinite." What Shakespeare is perhaps saying is that love is like a spring, ever flowing and constantly replenishing itself. Love stands apart in this way, because for almost everything else in the world, the more you give, the less you have. According to the *Kama Sutra*[132], the classical Hindu treatise on the art of making love, human sexual love is divine in its marvellous capacity to bring about a union of the male and female to propagate life.

A sexual smorgasbord

Dagmar O'Connor, in her book, *How to Make Love to the Same Person for the Rest of Your Life and Still Love It,*, introduces the concept of a sexual smorgasbord. Nature has given people pleasure in eating as an inducement to nourish themselves for self-preservation. Nature has also given us sexual pleasure as an inducement for mating in order to insure the preservation of the species. A smorgasbord is attractive because it provides a variety of foods. Similarly, a sexual smorgasbord is attractive because it provides variety in lovemaking and in the steps leading up to it.

Much of the allure of sex lies in its mystery. Women are abundantly endowed with it and men (sorry, fellows) possess it to a lesser degree. One way to unravel the secrets of sex is to explore the erogenous zones of the body, the spots in the body that are particularly sensitive sexually. Men's erogenous zones are mostly confined to the area around the groin. For women, they extend to many other parts of the body. In fact, a woman's entire body is an erogenous zone.

Yet it may be said in the words of Robert Nicoll Menie, "Fair was her sweet body, still fairer was her mind."

Why is sex like jazz?

If sex is so natural, why are there so many sex manuals?

Sophisticated lovers are not obsessed with techniques. They realize that in the heart of lovemaking, that which is natural and spontaneous is the best. They treat sex like jazz, music delightful in its creative improvisation while conveying a wide range of meanings. It is the absence of a scripted formula that provides pleasant surprises. Lovemaking may take place in unusual settings or in an adventurous way, such as in a canoe, during a thunderstorm, or while on a nature hike. Sex manuals flood the market. While they offer useful suggestions, some of the positions illustrated are nice to look at but difficult to execute. One needs the agility of an acrobat to engage in contorted positions. Acrobatic techniques in lovemaking could lessen the joy of sex.

III. Intellectual and aesthetic intimacy

Just as emotional intimacy leads to a union of hearts, intellectual intimacy leads to a union of minds. The two intimacies are interwoven. Sharing pleasant thoughts and engaging in spirited discussion is a banquet for the mind. It can create on earth a little bit of heaven. When two people become intellectually intimate, an exciting new world dawns upon them. Together they may gather glimpses of reality that they may not have grasped separately. Taken together, their ideas are richer because they are complementary. Thus, when Peter designs a vase, Paula may suggest that hollow spaces be made to enhance its beauty. Thanks to their joint efforts, the vase may become a work of art. Philosophically, Peter might think that within a man there lies a lion and a fox. Paula might think that within him there also lies a dove and a nightingale. Their composite views would hold that the proportion in which people display these qualities explains the diversity of their characters. Thus, people could be strong and cunning, peaceful and charming, to various degrees.

Peter and Paula may engage in spirited discussions about their friends, history, and politics. They may observe that while many people are good and many are great, few are both. These people are such a rare breed that they shine from afar like snowy mountaintops. We shall now specifically discuss the benefits of intellectual intimacy.

Explore the meaning of life

We best enjoy life when we give it meaning and purpose and when our endeavors are satisfying. While we can achieve this individually, it is better to have the mutual support of a loving companion. In union, the partners may discuss, as Edmund Burke[133] (1729–1797) wrote, that "we are thrust into this world without being asked and we shall be taken away from it without our assent." The choice is clear: an intense love for life becomes pressing when we realize that we are mortal. Wisdom tells us that as this earthly existence is all we have, we must try hard to enjoy it while it lasts.

Through intellectual intimacy, we may find some answers to these questions. Intimate dialogue could help us explore common strategies for achieving success, riches, and recognition. If these strategies work, they would offer satisfaction. To solidify this satisfaction, however, we must be mindful of the price we would have to pay.

Seek not endless joys

> *Sleep, riches and health to be truly enjoyed, must be interrupted.*[134]
> —*Johann Paul Friedrich Richter*[135] *(1763– 1825)*

Through intellectual intimacy, we must sort out the paradox that the frantic search for happiness may indeed cause unhappiness. Wisdom tells us that we cannot be perennially happy because it is unreal. The human heart is unable to accept uninterrupted happiness. George Bernard Shaw, in his play *Man and Superman*, wrote that "a lifetime of happiness!——no man could bear it; it would be hell on earth." Through intellectual intimacy, we are able to better understand the nature of life. We cannot pluck fragrant roses without being pricked by thorns, nor can we enjoy the spring of sweet content without facing the winter of discontent. We cannot interact with prudent and kind people without facing the unpleasantness of the stupid and unkind.

In better understanding, through intellectual intimacy, the nature of life, we are able to develop a higher tolerance for discouraging, disappointing, and depressing events. The principal cause of such events is the unpredictability and uncertainty of life. We do not know for sure what may happen during the next day, hour, or minute. Uncertainty follows us like our own shadow. The best we can do is to expect the unexpected. Life itself consists of a series of surprises.

Natural beauty is overwhelming. The artist tries to make it comprehensible by simplifying scenery in a portrait contained within a frame. It is the role of the artist to edit nature. That is why the portrait of scenery is contained within a frame.

In admiring nature, the lovers behave like artists. As we saw in the prologue, it is soothing to jointly observe a river and a mountain exist side by side as friendly neighbors. Charles Dickens wrote, "There is always a charm in nature and the possibilities for enjoying it are limitless."

Jointly admiring the masterpieces of great painters provides a rich, visual experience that stirs the soul. *The Scream*, by Edward Munch[136] (1863–1944), succeeds brilliantly in conveying the horror in a man's face. His cheeks are so sunken that he seems to cry out in pain. The eerie surroundings seem to suggest that the whole world is against him.

An intriguing challenge for the eye is Henry Rousseau's[137] (1844–1910) painting *The Dream*. It depicts a nude woman reclining over a velvet sofa, amidst the flora and fauna of a lush and exotic jungle. While the woman is sleeping peacefully, a lion is gently bending over to kiss her lips. Up in the sky is a solitary moon, casting its light on the entire scene. What is most striking about the painting is how the separate and incongruous parts have been brought together by the genius of the artist. The message is clear. There is harmony in the midst of incongruity.

The Scream, by Edward Munch. Notice the horror in the man's face.[138]

Through the works of Auguste Renoir[139] (1841–1919), partners have an opportunity to gather a glimpse of a genius. In the portrait of a man and a woman dancing, *Dance at Bougival,* Renoir was able to capture in an extraordinary way the movement, the rhythm, and even the music of the dance. Renoir stands singular among painters. To portray beautiful women he did not use models, as other painters did. Even the great Leonardo DaVinci[140] (1452–1519) had Madame del Giocondo pose for him, to capture her enigmatic smile in the *Mona Lisa*. Renoir did not portray women in his paintings as they looked in real life, but women yearned to look like the subjects in his paintings. According to Renoir's son, "The vision that the artist created was so enchanting" that after a while the women applied their makeup in such a way as to look like the women in the paintings.

Here is a challenge for partners to become more romantic by heightening their visual perceptions and creative talents. Through pleasant dialogue, design a collage from different elements. The collage may include pictures of children playing, adults laughing, animals running, birds flying, fires burning, and waters flowing. The examples from which you could select are infinite.

Miracles to behold

Sharing rich experiences about the wonders of nature is a sure way to enjoy aesthetic intimacy. The poet George Gordon, Lord Byron[141] (1788-1824) suggested "we find pleasure in the pathless wood and rapture on the lonely shores."[142] The Lebanese-American writer Kahil Gibran wished, "Let the earth delight to feel your bare feet and the wind long to play with your hair." Aesthetic intimacy strengthens the bond with our partner when we realize that we are one with nature. We share certain things, like protoplasm, in common with all life forms. Protoplasm is the same living substance found in all plants and animals from the tiny amoeba to the mighty blue whale.

A miracle to behold is how plants and animals adapt themselves to changes in the environment. Seasonal changes force them to adapt or perish. This is most noticeable in the massive migration of birds escaping from the cold to warmer climes. With amazing skill they fly over rivers and oceans, navigating through thunderstorms and fierce winds. En route they stop by the banks of rivers and lakes to feed and gather energy for their onward journey. Their flurry of activity at these stops is a spectacle well worth watching. In their new spring habitat, many of them engage in ritual courtship prior to mating. Fortunately for us, their "romantic" dances have been well captured on film, which are available in many libraries.

A slightly different pattern is found among mammals such as deer and elk. The males grow elegant antlers and engage in non-deadly combat to display their masculine strength and impress the females. In the animal world, the male is more attractive than the female. The lion is proud of its mane and the peacock of its plumage. They use them as adornments and as a form of sexual allure. In springtime reproduction becomes paramount in the animal kingdom. Among human beings, romance and courtship is also prominent, hence the popularity of June weddings in Western culture.

It would be sobering to comprehend through aesthetic intimacy, a supreme law of nature that all life forms must ensure the emergence of new life forms. Spring seems to be the favourite time for this function to occur, among both plants and animals. Though people are romantic at all seasons, spring seems to be the favourite time. This idea was well expressed by William Wordsworth[143] (1770-1850) when he wrote, "With the approach of spring, the fancy of many a young man turns to thoughts of love." Numerous are the poems and songs connecting love with the spring. Consider the imagery in this song:

> Remember little darling it was only late spring,
> when the mountain laurels were in bloom.
> We both strolled hand in hand down Lovers' Lane.
> Darling, how can you forget so soon?

Through aesthetic intimacy we can share the rich experience of how plants adapt themselves in the winter and the spring. Like some animals, many plants remain dormant in the winter. Their bark looks pale and devoid of any foliage; they look like skeletons. The plants seem to be biding their time for the winter to end. Plants welcome the coming of spring, and it affects them. They adapt themselves remarkably by absorbing the warm rays of the sun to acquire a new energy and vitality.

They put forth a new variety of blossoms, which are a festival of colors. The blossoms commence the process of reproduction, as they contain buds that will subsequently grow into fruits. The trees put on new leaves in a mass of green. But the green of no two trees is the same. The infinite beauty of the spring is only matched by the infinite beauty of the fall.

Marvels to fathom

Partners can obtain much joy in observing a fascinating feature of nature, such as how it has equipped birds to adapt to their environment so well. The beak is an important limb for birds. The heron's beak, for instance, helps it to seize fish and eel from the waters. The cuckoo's beak is suitable for picking up caterpillars. The parrot's beak is strong and sharp to crack seeds and cut up fruits. The woodpecker has a chisel-like beak that enables it to chop insects out of dead wood.

Birds of prey are specially adapted for hunting. Hawks, eagles, and owls have claws on their feet that enable them to seize prey and carry them afloat.

The osprey is a skilled fisherman. It dives into the water, grabs fish, and flies away. Intimately observing with our partner the marvellous adaptation of birds could lift our spirits like that of the soaring eagles.

It is a marvel to observe how birds lift off into the air, soar at great heights, and then land gracefully. They are light to defy gravity, yet strong to withstand the tremendous stress and strain on their bones and muscles. They have a tremendous sense of sight and balance to navigate through turbulent winds and to pass by treetops and mountains.

The feather is a remarkable instrument. Along with your partner, run your finger through a feather. Observe how it is almost weightless but still so strong and flexible. The forelimbs or arms act as wings, enabling the bird to soar and glide. A philosophical matter to discuss as a matter of aesthetic intimacy is, who designed the feather as an instrument of aeronautics?

"Queen of the Night"

The adaptation of plants to the environment is also a marvel to ponder. Cacti have developed special tuberous roots adapted for water storage. A famous cactus is the "Queen of the Night,", who's enlarged roots may weigh as much as twenty-five to thirty-five kilograms.

Plants that grow on rocks and by the mountainside send their roots through the cracks and into the underlying substrata. Just as water finds its way, roots seem to find their way to water. Beach plants are well adapted to survive in a harsh environment. They are deeply rooted in the soil and are capable of surviving salt water and severe drought.

Plants overcome serious barriers to survive and seem to have a mind of their own. The message that nature offers is very clear. When facing barriers to living, look for cracks and openings among them. They could provide us opportunities for living. Franklin Delano Roosevelt was crippled with polio, but that did not hold him back from becoming one of America's greatest presidents.

IV. Crisis and conflict intimacy

Living is like licking honey off a thorn

This same flower that smiles today, tomorrow shall be withering.⁻
Robert Hendrick

What was difficult to endure is sweet to recall. What was once a crisis may become a triumph. And sometimes our sorrows may turn into joys.

How numerous are the examples of people stricken with near fatal illnesses who remained resilient and fully recovered. In each of these cases, the abiding support of an intimate partner, a family member, or a friend helped in recovering from tragedy. A crisis reveals the true character of people. While many would wine and dine with you in good times, they sometimes become distant in bad times. A person who is intimately involved with you during a crisis displays several marvelous qualities: loving, loyal, reliable, and empathetic.

The crisis intimacy may produce a bond of love so strong that it cannot be easily torn asunder. The partners may consider each other as a gift from the gods. Crisis intimacy is not merely an idealised form of relationship; it has actually happened in real life. A number of cases have been reported of a spouse or partner risking his or her life in order to donate a kidney or liver to a loved one.

Kahlil Gibran was perhaps referring to crisis intimacy when he wrote that you may forget the person with whom you have laughed, but never the person with whom you have wept. Through crisis intimacy is born great tenderness that enriches the mind and heart.

As Louis Adamic[144] (1899–1951) said, "Living is like licking honey off a thorn." Life can be sweet but also bitter. A child's smile, a walk by the river, and a decent income can gladden the heart, but in the midst of it all disaster may strike. Life indeed is a pendulum between a smile and a tear.[145]

In these times it is consoling to rely on a loving partner, to whom we may say in the words of Sir Walter Scott, "When pain and anguish wring my brow, a ministering angel art thou." What the partners offer most is hope. They may further say to each other, in the words of Victor Hugo, "Press on: better days await thee."

Reconciling romance with finance
> *Heiresses are always beautiful.*
> —*John Dryden*[146](*1631–1700*)

"I am a wonderful housekeeper," Zsa Zsa Gabor once said. "Every time I divorce a man, I keep his house."

All women are not as lucky as you, Ms. Gabor. Even among the best of relationships, honest differences of opinion might arise over finances. Critical choices have to be made whether to spend or invest and where to invest. Just as one fly spoils an ointment, so to can one fight spoil a pleasant mood.

It is nice to imagine that all that is mine is thine, but that is idealism. Lips that are rosy must be fed. Practically speaking, there is a need to hammer out a consensus over finances. A starting point may be financial planning for the near and distant future, with detailed budgeting for the most efficient use of resources. A couple may both have a joint account and a separate account and use them according to a formula achieved through mutual dialogue. Though not easy, romance must be reconciled with finance.

As a humorist said, "As life is short, the sooner we enjoy our money the better."

We must avoid the pitfalls of viewing genuine intimacy in an idealized manner. We cannot hope to sleep on a bed of roses. Barriers to genuine intimacy will arise, but generally they are not insurmountable. Learning to overcome or minimize conflicts strengthens a union. Having gone through a crucible of fire, the partners may better understand each other's shortcomings and their respective strengths. It is important, however, to speedily allow the scars to heal. Remember, you can only be hurt if you care. We shall discuss four barriers to genuine intimacy—frustration, perceptions, pride, and prejudice—and present ways to overcome them.

From frustration to inspiration

Frustration is a common human emotion. It affects people of all ages. An infant is frustrated when there is too much light. A senior is frustrated when there is too little light. Failure to satisfy a want or need results in internal stress, ranging from mild annoyance to irritability.

Frustration is a part of life and it is inevitable. It could occur when one is torn between two desirable goals. For instance, a man may have to make a choice whether to go to graduate school or to get married. A woman may have to make a choice whether to continue her career or have a baby.

If a partner allows his or her level of frustration to accumulate, it could lead to too much stress and tension. The partner may become aggressive, which is a road to conflict. Partners need to be ever watchful not to permit their levels of frustration to reach boiling point. It is vital that we nip it in the bud. As frustration is an unavoidable reality of life, we need to build a defense mechanism that will permanently protect us.

Developing a high tolerance for frustration is like armor that protects us against life's many irritants. Amidst traffic jams, long queues, the law's delays, and the awkwardness of some people, we need to remain cool and calm. The graceful attitude is infectious to our partners. The synergy of both could help them to triumph over their frustration.

Harmonize different perceptions

Perception refers to the knowledge we acquire through our senses. Thus, in the following diagram, our visual perception indicates that the top line is longer when, in fact, it is the same length as the line below it. Our perception of things is sometimes unreliable.

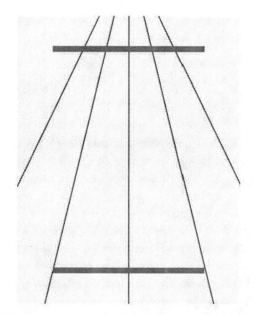

Our perception is sometimes unreliable.

Differences in perception could lead to tension and even conflict. Our perception of life could be wrong. We think a bird in a cage sings when in fact it may be crying. What is paradoxical is that when clashes occur, both partners may be right in their own way. What, then, are the causes for tension, and how can they be eased?

Misunderstandings cause honest differences in perception. Psychologically, it has been well established that no two people view the same phenomenon or event in the same way. Thus, John and Jean wearing identical clothes go for a walk. While the same breeze blows over them, Jean feels cold and John feels warm. Both of them are honest, though they have opposite opinions.

The two partners may view life in different ways, shaped by their different backgrounds and unique experiences. John may have suffered from an unhappy family background, whereas Jean hails from a happy family. Furthermore, their education, friends, pastimes, and other social influences could be different. All these factors taken together have shaped their personalities, ideas, values, attitudes, and priorities.

When differences arise and each party sticks to his or her own rigid view, then clashes are inevitable. What is most needed to clear differences in perception is the quality of empathy. Each party attempts to understand the other by putting him or herself in the other's shoes. When there is empathy, divergent views are not divisive but complementary. They enrich a relationship.

Pride and prejudice

> *The mind unlearns with difficulty what it has long learned.*
> *—Seneca[147] (ca. 4 BC–AD 65)*

Jane Austen (1775–1815), who was considered one of England's great novelists, echoed this insight of Seneca in a stylish way. Her works often revolved around the delicate business of providing husbands for marriageable daughters. She's particularly noted for her vivid descriptions, lively interplay of character, and superb sense of irony.

In her classic novel *Pride and Prejudice*, she presents a vivid story about a romance that was once lost and later regained. She weaves together a telling tale about the interplay of two powerful emotions in the stormy relationship of Elizabeth and Darcy. Initially, both individuals display mutual attraction. Darcy is a dashing, wealthy young man of aristocratic lineage. Elizabeth is a country girl with four sisters, with whom she has a raucous relationship over the selection of potential bridegrooms.

The relationship between Darcy and Elizabeth is turbulent. Darcy is proud of his nobility and has an air of superiority about him. Though he is fond of Elizabeth, his pride stands in the way of truly displaying his love. Elizabeth, too, likes Darcy but is turned off by his pride and is blind to his virtues. She is prejudiced against him. They did not realize that one pardons to the extent that one loves.

Then a marvelous turnaround occurs. A relationship that was once frigid begins to thaw when a little openness and understanding emerges between the two. As they get closer, Darcy's pride gradually fades, and so does Elizabeth's prejudice. They see each other in true light and they fall in love.

Austen's story illustrates that negative emotions could destroy budding flowers of love. Pride, as we saw in Chapter 1, is based on folly and could have unwelcome results. Prejudice, on the other hand, is a little more complex because, at least to a minor degree, it is universal. Prejudice comes from the Latin word *prejudicium*, which means "prejudgement."

It is inevitable that we engage in prejudgement because life is complicated and we cannot afford the luxury of studying an issue in detail to arrive at a sound judgement. Necessity compels us to make instant judgements, which are sometimes wrong. This is quite acceptable as long as we realize that tentative judgements could be wrong. Prudence demands that we review our initial judgements.

Let your aesthetic experiences grow so pleasant that you can say to your partner, in the words of Conrad Aiken, "The bread I ate with you was more than bread, and the wine I drank with you was more than wine."

V. Communication intimacy

The essence of good communication is to satisfy the deep urge among human beings to be recognized and appreciated.

An ability to explain what we really mean and feel is an important part of good communication. The other part lies in understanding what our partner is trying to tell us.

A smooth dialogue provides an opportunity for free expression, which is a deep human desire that must be satisfied. A sincere expression is a mark of genuine intimacy, a state in which the partners are able to touch each other's soul. And as we saw in Chapter 1, baring one's soul, at least partially, is an antidote to loneliness and anxiety. Samuel Taylor Coleridge wrote, "That what comes from the heart, that alone goes to the heart." [148]

Genuine companionship achieved through genuine communication may be more effective than any pill in easing tensions because it adds pleasantness to life. The human spirit hungers for intimate fellowship.

We shall now discuss three specific ways how we may achieve intimacy through communication.

Perfect the art of listening

A humorist wrote that a man has one tongue but two ears. He should therefore listen twice as much as he speaks. Except for the humor, this statement sounds extreme. We cannot listen to people who talk too much because they may think too little. Our partner, however, is special. Readily, we should lend our ears.

Listening is an art, and like any art it needs to be cultivated. A first step is to create a climate for pleasant conversation. Sincerity and sensitivity to the feelings of our partner is a must, and so is a keen interest in the subject under discussion.

A golden rule in good conversation is to let your partner complete a train of thought. Frequent interruptions are rude. Occasional interruptions are in order, particularly if the partner tends to be longwinded. We must not be guilty of the same offense and know when to stop. A common mistake to avoid is constant repetition. It makes the conversation boring. Some interruptions are natural and, in fact, spice up the conversation.

A common problem to be avoided is boredom arising out of the monotony of the subject. We may overcome this barrier by discussing a wide range of topics so that we have plenty to talk about. If a conversation is too long or too mundane, gently switch to a topic that is mutually acceptable.

The skillful use of words is an effective tool for smooth conversation. It is important to note that sometimes men and women have different meanings for the same word. This is true even for intimate partners. The different interpretations that men and women give to the same vocabulary makes it appear, according to author John Gray, that "men are from Mars and women are from Venus."

Some men would be proud to consider themselves macho if that signifies being assertive. Some women, however, may consider it to be male chauvinism. Some men may think that gentleness is synonymous with weakness, whereas some women may treat a person with this quality as every bit a gentlemen.

The essence of good communication is to satisfy the deep craving within us to be recognized and appreciated. This craving is unique to human beings. As Blaise Pascal wrote, "No animal admires another animal."

Expression through body language

> *The body says what words cannot.*
> —*Martha Graham*[149] *(1894–1991)*

The noted choreographer was referring to ballet, in which the body is trained to display a variety of expressions. With graceful movements the dancer narrates a story, leaps for joy, drowns in sorrow, and floats with excitement.

While our body cannot match the elegance of a dancer, we can nevertheless convey a variety of meanings persuasively. Our physical gestures show to what degree we are interested and receptive. Nodding the head in agreement, counting the points on the fingers, and leaning forward to hear better are familiar techniques. And when giving advice, let it be gentle like the snow. The softer it falls, the longer it dwells.

Occasionally, whisper something into the ear. It could be very effective.

Mutual musical appreciation

After food, clothing, and shelter, music is another vital need and the universal language of humanity. It conveys meaning and emotion even without words.

Through joint hearing, the partners share rich sensory experiences. A welcome relief from the cacophony of the noisy world is to listen to the three elemental sounds of nature: rain, wind, and ocean. There is an appealing rhythm to all of them, which softens the harsh tones of traffic and machines.

Sharing the experience of listening to the music of songbirds is thrilling to the ear. Early morning is the best time to listen to a chorus of tunes near woodland or a bird sanctuary. If this is not possible, listen to recorded music in the luxury of your home. It would be enjoyable for the partners to identify the unique sounds from a variety of birds. How do they compare with one another with regard to musical texture, timbre, or pitch? What sounds distinguish their mating calls and the assertion of their territory?

While engaged in joint music appreciation, the partners may have different interpretations. Sharing them provides an intensely enjoyable way of communication. While one partner may keep count of the rhythm, the other may concentrate on the melody. Together, they can discuss how well they harmonize.

Some lyrics are inspiring and contain a certain philosophical message.

"Everything is beautiful in its own way, like the starry summer skies and the snow covered winter's day."
(Ray Stephens, "Everything is Beautiful", 1970)

"People who need people are the luckiest people in the world."
(Barbra Streisand, "People", 1964).

Lyrics offer hope and comfort, as in this song from the film *Doctor Zhivago*:

"Someday my love, there will be songs to sing,
although the snow covers the hope of spring."
(MGM Studio Orchestra, "Lara's Theme", 1965)

A further opportunity for sweet dialogue is to follow the story in a song:

"On a cold and grey Chicago morn, another little baby child is born
in the ghetto ... and his mama cries ..."
(Elvis Presley, "In The Ghetto", 1969)

Here is another story contained in a song:

"Down the road I look and there runs Mary,
hair of gold and lips like cherries;
It's good to touch the green, green grass of home."
(Tom Jones, "Green, Green Grass of Home", 1966)

Idolization is an important part of lyrics:

"You touch my hand and I am a king.
Your kiss to me is worth a fortune."
(Elvis Presley, "The Wonder of You", 1970)

Sometimes a song has a clear message, such as this one:

"Life is a cabaret, old chum,
Only a cabaret, old chum,
So come to the cabaret."
(Louis Armstrong, "Cabaret", 1968)

Following the imagery in lyrics is a lot of fun:

"Something in your eyes was so inviting.
Something in your smile was so exciting."
(Frank Sinatra, "Strangers in the Night", 1966)

Lyrics may contain great pledges of love:

"If I were to live forever and all my dreams come true, my memories
of love will be of you."
(John Denver and Placido Domingo, "Perhaps Love", (1984)

"My love is brighter than the brightest star that shines every night
above...

and nothing in this world can change my love."
(Petula Clark, "My Love", 1965)

Another enjoyable experience for partners is to listen to lovely instrumental music, such as Handel's "Largo." As everything that is thought and felt cannot be conveyed through words, music expresses our innermost feelings of love, joy, grief and loneliness. It stirs the soul when it is inspiring, comforting, loving and soothing.

Share rich personal experiences

A joy that is shared is a joy made double. "The joyfulness of people prolongeth their life," says the Bible. Sharing sensual pleasure offers a fine opportunity for enhancing romantic love. A feast for the eyes, a lingering melody, a fragrant flower, a bout of wine tasting, and the touch of bare skin—each radiates warmth and puts a couple into ecstatic delight.

In exchanging gifts, what matters most is not the gift of the lover but the love of the giver. Your presents need not be expensive perfumes. Instead, present your lover with fresh flowers, leaves, and branches and say to him or her, "My heart is still beating for you." Perform little acts of kindness: remember your partner's birthday but forget her age. Have regular candlelight dinners without waiting for a power failure. Surprise your partner with marks of affection at unlikely places and times, such as a pajama party, a secret hideaway, or a private box at a sporting event. An impromptu love letter has a magical effect.

Here is a sample:

My Dearest Sakuntala,

Even one minute spent with you gives me sixty seconds of happiness.

What have you done to me? You have made a poet of me, which no other woman has ever done. Every passing day you are becoming more loveable and more adorable. You have provoked within me very tender feelings for you. Perish the thought that you have to fear anything. I will treat you with great respect and relate to you very tenderly. I will assure you a lot of freedom, free as the wind blows and as the grass grows. Only permit me to love you …

On this special day, I pledge to you to make your life sweeter, stronger, and fuller. May you enjoy the supreme happiness in the conviction that you are intensely loved.

You are to me a bright torch, exposing the hypocrisy of men and the darker side of society. Your goodness touches me. Your mystique

inspires me. Your beauty fascinates me. Your kindness wins my love.
I constantly admire your pictures, but the best part of your beauty no picture could express. I alone have discovered it.

Oscar Wilde said that woman is man's confusion; you are my consolation.
My deepest love,
Gopalan

My favorite love story is that of Dante and Beatrice. It was completed in 1321 shortly before Dante died, but it is still fresh and lively today. It was the genius of Dante to set the love story in the background of prudery and hypocrisy in medieval times. Dante narrates his story in beautiful poetry called *The Divine Comedy*. He walks through hell and is guided by the Roman poet Virgil. In heaven he is escorted by his beloved Beatrice. While in hell, he is shocked to meet popes and cardinals who confessed to him that while on earth they seldom practiced what they preached. In heaven he was escorted by Beatrice, who claimed she was misjudged on earth because she was attractive and unmarried. Nevertheless, she was well known for her charitable work. Most surprisingly, the very clerics who condemned her morality also sought her friendship. She had a special bond with Dante, who idolized her in his work. What earned her a place in heaven was her magnanimity on earth.

Erotometer: A technique for the measurement of genuine intimacy
Below is a list of items concerning marital or romantic love. Please respond to all of them on the basis of your feelings. Please rate yourself as strong or weak on the following points.
In your relationship with your partner would you be willing and able to:

- Overlook shortcomings
- Respect the other's expectations
- Show fidelity
- Want to be with the other often
- Settle conflicts amicably
- Feel intellectually intimate
- Feel emotionally intimate
- Feel physically intimate
- Share ethical convictions

- Promote a feeling of security
- Support the other in times of crisis
- Share decision-making responsibility
- Show appreciation on a regular basis
- Listen to what your partner is saying
- Express a need and a want for your partner

If you have more strengths than weaknesses, the state of your relationship is healthy. The erotometer is not a mathematical formula, but it is a broad indicator of the state of a relationship.

Try not to question your partner's judgment. Remember, your partner did choose you.

The seven intimacies could in combination present you *flashes of wisdom and moments of delight.*

They also remind us that love is something we can leave behind when we die.

Paradoxes to ponder

> Absence becomes the greatest presence.[150]
> --May Sarton

> In love, two beings become one and yet remain two.[151]
> --Erich Fromm

> Only love can be divided endlessly and still not diminish[152]
> --Anne Morrow Lindbergh

> Where love is concerned, too much is not even enough!
> --Pierre De Beaumarchais

> Families with babies and families without babies are sorry for each other.
> --Thomas Fuller

114. George Eliot, George Eliot's Works (Estes and Lauriat, 1894), 53.

115. Aiken was an American poet, short story writer, critic, and novelist. Most of his work reflects his intense interest in psychoanalysis and the development of identity.

116. Halford Edward Luccock, *Marching Off the Map: And Other Sermons* (Harper, 1952), p.34.

117. Maturin Murray Ballou, *Notable Thoughts about Women: A Literary Mosaic* (Houghton, Mifflin and Company, 1882), 184.

118. A preeminent English author, Dickens was imprisoned for failure to pay a debt. He used his many unhappy experiences as a foundation for his famous novels.

119. Greene was an English playwright, novelist, short story writer, travel writer, and critic. Graham Greene, *The Heart of the Matter* (Viking Press, 1948), 84.

120. Excerpt from "A Daisy a Day," Jud Strunk, 1972.

121. American actress who played the heroine role in *Ship of Fools*.

122. He devised a new model of the atom by applying quantum theory.

123. An English writer remembered for his humanistic essays and literary criticism, Hazlitt is often viewed as the greatest English literary critic after Samuel Johnson. William Hazlitt, *William Ernest Henley, The Collected Works of William Hazlitt* (J.M. Dent & Co.; McClure, Phillips & Co, 1903), 77..

124. A French novelist who is most famous for having written 'Gigi'.

125. A noted Canadian author of non-fiction, especially Canadian history.

126. W Lambert Gardiner, *A History of Media* (Trafford Publishing, 2006), 80.

127. Suggestions taken from Godek, *1001 Ways to be Romantic*, 2000.

128. Often referred to simply as Dr. Johnson, he was one of England's greatest literary figures: a poet, essayist, biographer, lexicographer, and often considered the finest critic of English literature. Samuel Johnson, *The works of Samuel Johnson* (Project Gutenberg, 1823), 156.

129. Comfort was best known for writing *The Joy of Sex*. Alex Comfort, *The New Joy of Sex* (Pocket Books, 1972), 9.

130. DeAngelis, *Real Moments for Lovers*, Barbara De Angelis Ph.D. Dell Publshing, New York First Editon 1995.

131. *Romeo and Juliet* is a famous play by William Shakespeare concerning the fate of two young, star-crossed lovers. William Shakespeare, *William Shakespeare* (Barron's Educational Series, 2002), 143.

132. An ancient Indian text widely considered to be the standard work on love in Sanskrit literature. The earliest version appeared in the first century BC.

133. Burke was an Anglo-Irish statesman, author, orator, political theorist, and philosopher.

134. John Cook, *The Book of Positive Quotations* (Fairview Press, 2007), p.688.

135. Richter, a German writer, was best known for his humorous novels.

136. Munch was a Norwegian Symbolist painter and pioneer of Expressionistic art, the tendency of an artist to distort reality for an emotional effect.

137. Rousseau was a French post-Impressionist painter. Ridiculed during his life, he later was recognized as a self-taught genius whose works are of high artistic quality.

138. This copy of *The Scream* is from is from www.angelo.edu.

139. A French artist, Renoir was a leading painter in the development of Impressionism.

140. DaVinci was an Italian scientist, mathematician, engineer, inventor, anatomist, painter, sculptor, architect, musician, and writer. He was perhaps the most versatile genius in all history

141. Byron, an English Romantic poet, was described by a critic as "mad, bad, and dangerous to know." He almost certainly suffered from bipolar disorder, which was the source of his tempestuous moods.

142. Joseph Cross, *Portraiture and Pencilings of the Late Mrs. L.A.L. Cross* (A.H. Ford, Printed at the office of the Nashville and Louisville Christian Advocate. John Lellyett, printer, 1851), 241.

143. Wordsworth, a British poet, is credited with ushering in the English Romantic Movement with the publication of *Lyrical Ballads* (1798), in collaboration with Samuel Taylor Coleridge.

144. Adamic was a Slovenian-American author and translator. Louis Adamic, *The Native's Return: An American Immigrant Visits Yugoslavia and Discovers...* (Harper & Brothers, 1934), 67.

145. Adapted from Lord Byron's *Childe Harold's Pilgrimage*, Canto iv, stanza 9.

146. Dryden was an English poet, satirist, dramatist, and critic. John Dryden, *The Works of John Dryden* (University of California Press, 1974), 13.

147. Seneca was a Roman philosopher, statesman, dramatist, and, in one work,a humorist.

148. Samuel Taylor Coleridge, *The Complete Works of Samuel Taylor Coleridge: With an Introductory Essay* (Harper & Brothers, 1853), 472.

149. Graham was an American dancer and choreographer and one of the foremost pioneers of modern dance.

150. May Sarton, 1912–1955, an American poet and novelist.

151. Erich Pinchas Fromm (1900–1980) was an internationally renowned German-American social psychologist.

152. Anne Morrow Lindbergh, *Dearly Beloved: A Theme and Variations* (Harcourt, Brace & World, 1962), p.133.

Chapter 4
Be Ever Young In Spirit

Chapter 4
Be Ever Young in Spirit

More than two thousand years ago, the Chinese philosopher Mencius[153] wrote, "A man of true greatness never loses the heart of a child."[154] He noted that some of the finest qualities of human nature are found in children in great abundance. The secret to feeling and staying young all our lives is to boldly adopt childlike qualities.

A high sense of wonder and curiosity, a capacity for fun and play, and an ability to be free of worry are some of the hallmarks of a youthful spirit. Filled with this spirit, we can enjoy the boundless energy of children and their limitless enthusiasm for life.

I. Discovering a youthful spirit

Children as models

The school of life has many stages, and we enter each stage as a novice. To do well in this school, we should approach each stage like a child entering a new grade. By adopting such an approach, eminent men and women have led creative lives. They were active and vigorous right up to their nineties and some even beyond one hundred years. A famous example is the brilliant scientist Isaac Newton, who died at the age of eighty-four. He viewed himself as "a boy playing on the seashore ... now and then finding a smooth pebble."

In our own time, George Bernard Shaw, the playwright, enjoyed life and was mentally alert until age ninety-seven. Bertrand Russell, the philosopher, led life to the fullest until ninety-six. Martha Graham danced her way through life until age eighty-eight. The actor George Burns was a centenarian and had people laughing until the end.

In almost all walks of life, there are people who are energized with a youthful spirit. They view life afresh, with joy and excitement.

It is fascinating to observe the tremendous satisfaction that grandparents enjoy in watching the world through the eyes of their grandchildren. Children know how to enjoy the present. They do not worry about the past or future. Adults, however, do not have the luxury of being unconcerned about the future.

In simple but profound words, Jesus Christ said, "Let the little children come to me, and do not hinder them, for the kingdom of heaven belongs to such as these."[155] It would be very wise to hearken to these words.

A sense of wonder

The ancient Greeks claimed that there were seven wonders in the world. To a child's imagination there might as well be seventy wonders. Children love to hear astonishing stories, such as the one related by Dr. Paul Handford, a biology professor at the University of Western Ontario. He claimed that songbirds, like sparrows, sing only at dawn and dusk because the songs are conveyed at these times with greater clarity.[156]

Children are fascinated by nature. They marvel at the stripes of a tiger and the mane of a lion. They love to climb hills and jump from trees. They wonder why the sky is blue, why apples are red, and why the grass is green. They also ask how a single cell becomes a beautiful baby in only forty weeks.

This childlike wonder among adults has been the source of much imagination, enabling them to probe the most distant stars in the most distant galaxies. Thomas Carlyle wrote that wonder is the beginning of wisdom.

A sense of wonder fascinated me as a child. I recall how excited I was when taught about bioluminescence—the phenomenon of plants and animals emitting light. I observed that fireflies emitted a type of cold light. I also read that certain fungi, like mold, glow in the dark.

Another feature that astounded me was the role of carnivorous plants, like the Venus flytrap, which trap and digest insects.

As a mature adult I would wander in the woods and reflect on the questions posed by Omar Khayyam: "Where is the coolness when no cold wind blows, and where is the music when the lute lies low?"[157]

A sense of curiosity

Children are ever curious. They want to know everything about everything. They pose questions that baffle the adult mind. How does the sap climb up to the top of a tree? Why did the mastodons of North America vanish? More mature children may be curious to know why a strong wind does not push down a tall building. They listen in amazement to the explanation that most tall buildings are constructed of steel beams or reinforced concrete. These materials are flexible—that is, they can bend slightly without breaking. When strong winds blow, the steel and concrete buildings give way to the force of the wind by bending a little. They want to know how the chameleon changes its colors and the salamander regenerates a severed limb, and why the platypus, which is a mammal, also lays eggs. Finally, they may ask philosophical questions, such as, "Why do people kill people?" In soliciting answers, children soak up knowledge like a sponge.

If this childlike curiosity extends to adults, it produces great accomplishments. They invigorate life and make one feel youthful at any age.

II. Sustaining a youthful spirit

We shall now discuss some other childlike qualities. They include imagination, open-mindedness, resilience, and pure happiness. These astonishing qualities infuse children with so much energy and zest for life. Fun-loving children are very receptive to the gentleness of adults. Your child may do almost anything for you if you promise to play with her, for instance.

The genius of childhood

Ashley Montagu, an American social scientist, has contributed immensely to the study of children and their potential. His words have provided much inspiration for this book. One profound concept he presented in his book *Growing Young* was that of the "genius of childhood." He argued that, in order for adults to recapture their youth, they first need to recapture their childhood spirit. [158]

Imagination and open-mindedness

When adults display youthful expression, it provokes within them a rich imagination. Like a child, the adult forms mental images of reality. This can best be seen in the paintings of both age groups. When a child paints a picture of a rainbow or a flower, he draws upon his own imagery. So does an artist, whether it's Van Gogh[159] (1853–1890) or Monet[160] (1840–1926). In this respect, the artist resembles the child. For this reason, William Wordsworth wrote that the "child is the father of man."[161] Imitating childlike qualities makes an adult feel perennially young. Again we turn to Montagu, who argued, "Childhood is the period of maximum creativity."[162] It arises from the elation the child feels when interacting with adults who are loving and playful.

The child loves to daydream and engage in fantasy. This childlike quality, when continued in adulthood, results in acts of creation that are of a fantastic proportion. Much of our theater, film, dance, and visual art are built on fantasy. The whole of Walt Disney World is based on imagination, where adults acquire as much delight as children. When adults engage in creative activity, they put on a youthful countenance that could long linger with them.

A person remains ever young if he is open to new ideas and new experiences. His openness provides a conduit for a flow of fresh thought that nourishes his mind. If he constantly renews himself, there is little room for boredom. He grows mentally and emotionally, which is a sign of life and vitality.

One of the loveliest things in this world is to observe how freely children accept new phenomena without preconceived notions. They are, in certain respects, more objective than some adults. In a multicultural setting, children easily form friendships with other children who are culturally different. When adults value open-mindedness, exciting new frontiers await them. As Michel Montaigne[163] (1533–1592) wrote, "The beautiful souls are they that are universal, open and ready for all things."[164]

Though open-mindedness is a priceless asset, sometimes it begins to wane in adulthood. Unhealthy social factors, like the prejudices of society, may push the young adult to become less open or even closed-minded. The free circulation of ideas is restricted, resulting in hardening of the mind. Montagu labeled this condition as *psychosclerosis,* a state similar to arteriosclerosis, which is the hardening of arteries caused by restrictions to the free circulation of blood.

The best safeguard against psychosclerosis is to cultivate an open mind and sustain it until the end of our days. Remember, the human mind is like a parachute—it functions only when it opens.

Having an open mind helps me look at people and events more objectively. It ensures that my misjudgements are minimized. Open-mindedness is an excellent attitude with which you can finesse your judgment.

Resilience and pure happiness

To feel and act young we need to be like children, resilient in mind and body. Resilience is the ability to recover or bounce back from the stresses and strains of life. Children possess this ability to an astonishing degree. In war-torn areas, they suffer sheer fright from bombings. But within a short time they may end up playing in a crater using discarded shrapnel as toys.

Adults, too, display this childlike quality. Remarkable individuals have bounced back, turning failures into successes, setbacks into triumphs, and ill health into good health. The late Norman Cousins and Geraldine Ferraro, for example, conquered their cancers and went on to lead fruitful lives. The striking feature about resilience is tenacity—the capacity to never give up even in the face of adversity. You are ever youthful by being ever resilient.

The crowning glory of the youthful spirit is the capacity to enjoy pure happiness. This happens during early childhood, when children fully enjoy life, free of all concerns. It is, of course, easy for them to do so because they bear little responsibility. If, however, adults could recapture some of this pure happiness, they could feel young and exuberant.

Regretfully for adults, as Miguel de Cervantes[165] (1547–1616) wrote, happiness seldom comes in pure form. It is often tempered and mixed with a tinge of distress. Thus, in modern times, the joy of finding a fine job is lessoned by the anxiety of being on probation.

The key to being in a state of pure happiness is to draw a balance between being indifferent to the future and worrying about it to excess. Children are largely unconcerned about life's uncertainties. Adults do not have this luxury, but they still obtain much satisfaction from the simple pleasures of life. It is wonderful to be like a child, to play and laugh, sing and dance, and engage in spontaneous behavior.

To be endowed with the marvelous qualities of children provides us with *flashes of wisdom and moments of delight.*

III. A path to health and vigor

Recapture a younger age

Growth is a sign of life, and anyone who does not grow declines. Physically, there are limits to our growth on reaching adulthood, but mentally and emotionally, we can continue to grow immensely.

A youthful mind is a great asset in helping one achieve youthful vigor. The workings of the mind have a tremendous impact on the body. Olympic athletes perform wondrously when intense mental training presages their intense physical training, for instance.

One way to achieve a youthful mind and body is to think about our age in a fresh and unusual manner. This book draws certain ideas from the Indian scientist Deepak Chopra. He has presented an interesting concept called the "biological age."[166] It refers to "the optimum level to which the body can attain good health and fitness."

From the perspective of health, we should not place too much emphasis on our calendar age. If we are thirty years of age, the only real meaning of this is that the earth has simply circled the sun thirty times since we were born. Our biological age is of much greater personal relevance because it actually reveals to what extent we feel younger or older than our calendar age.

Chopra presents a set of objective criteria to gauge "biological age,"[167] with sixteen different measures (for a full review, see Appendix A). While a few, like aerobic activity and muscular strength, can be subject to self-test, the rest of the measures should be tested with the help of a physician.

Here is a sample of some of Chopra's sixteen measures:

- Aerobic capacity
- Blood pressure
- Body fat

- Bone density
- Cholesterol and lipid levels
- Hormonal levels

The better scores one obtains in these measures, the better the chances of feeling and acting younger. Chopra claims that one could feel younger by about twenty years. What is most promising is that even if the measures are not fully achieved, one can work diligently to improve upon them. Thus, a sixty-year-old would have the youthful vigor of a forty-year-old.

To discover ways to glow with youthful spirit is a sign of wisdom, which also adds delight to life.

It is within our power to grow younger and live longer. What we need is the will to do it. Though we cannot live forever, there is evidence that we have the potential to live beyond the age of 110 (see "Let centenarians point the way" later in this chapter). Freud's claim that "anatomy is destiny" is only partly true.

Clearing arteries

We shall now discuss how to shape the body to resemble that of a younger person by examining the connection between the mind and body.

The human body consists of billions of cells. The condition of every part of the body is determined by the condition of each of its cells. Every day, millions of them decay and die and are replaced by new ones. The body's capacity to constantly renew itself is remarkable.

Minimizing cellular damage and maximizing cellular renewal should together make up our master strategy to attain youthful vigour. We accomplish this by limiting the damaging effects of what are known as free radicals. These are "highly charged, rapidly moving molecular fragments that harm healthy cells," according to Dr. Timothy Smith, an American biochemist.[168]

Modern researchers, such as Dr. Smith, believe that free radicals have the potential to damage the nucleus of our cells. This, in turn, leads to abnormal and disorganized proliferation. If the ravaging effects of free radicals are not neutralized, they lead to severe health problems, such as cancer, atherosclerosis, and cardiac ailments.

The toxic effect of free radicals can be controlled both internally and externally. Internally, it is possible to minimize your intake of products that contain free radicals, such as additives, excess alcohol, saturated fats, and herbicides. External factors that are a source of free radicals are pollutants, chemical solvents, pesticides, radiation from the sun, radon gas, and medical and dental X-rays.

We can combat them and protect our cells by having a high consumption of foods rich in antioxidants, which are "the workhorses of the body's healing system and should form an essential part of one's daily diet."[169]

Antioxidant nutrients are found in vitamins A, C, and E; in minerals such as copper, selenium, zinc; and in certain fatty and amino acids. A variety of foods provide these nutrients. Among grains, the best are rye, wheat, oats, millet, brown rice, and corn. A variety of beans, like lentils, chickpeas, and green peas, are a fine source of nourishment. Similarly, fresh vegetables are bountiful in fiber. Eating a variety is best, ranging from squash and spinach to broccoli and eggplant.

Many nutritionists urge us to minimize animal products. Fish and poultry are preferable to red meat, and low-fat milk and cheese are preferable to the regular products. Similarly, nutritionists strongly suggest the moderate consumption of products containing white sugar and white flour. Add spice to life by flavoring your foods with cardamom, cayenne, cinnamon, clover, fenugreek, nutmeg, sage, and turmeric. Spices improve digestion, speed up metabolism, and are a rich source of antioxidants.

In conclusion, we may state that the more antioxidants we have in our system, the better our chances of staying healthy and youthful.

We have discussed many solid foods that are vital to consume. This is a good time to make an important point about liquids. For good health, it is absolutely essential to drink about eight glasses of water a day. As 70 percent of the body consists of water, it acts as a medium for the body to perform its many functions. It transports oxygen and nutrients to every cell and washes away toxins. It helps digestion and converts food into energy. It lubricates the eyes and spinal cord and nourishes the skin and purifies it. When these functions are not performed due to dehydration, a range of symptoms may arise.

For the body to be well tuned, it is critical that it retains water or remains hydrated. Drinks that promote hydration are milk, fruit and vegetable juices, and herbal tea. Coffee, beer, and alcohol consumed immoderately may lead to dehydration.

Improving metabolism
Diogenes (412–323 BC) was born in Sinope, in modern-day Turkey. He was the leading exponent of the school of thought called the Cynics. They

were noted for questioning everything, a critical attitude that prevails to this day.

When Diogenes was asked what the best time for supper is, he replied, "If you are a rich man, whenever you please, and if you are a poor man, whenever you can." [170]

A fellow Greek, Hippocrates[171] (460–370 BC), believed that food is medicine. He held that the body must be treated as a whole and not just as a series of parts. He also advocated the natural healing process of rest, a good diet, fresh air, and cleanliness.

In 1733, Benjamin Franklin said that "to lengthen thy life, lessen thy meals." A fresh way of looking at food improves our metabolism, which is the rate at which the body burns calories. Specifically, we benefit from a new scientific theory called the glycemic index. It is a measure of the speed at which food is digested and converted into glucose. The body needs glucose for energy, but excess glucose is converted into fat. Dr. David Jenkins, a Canadian nutritionist, describes the index "not as a diet but as a way of thinking."[172]

A winning strategy for eating well is to be more selective in choosing carbohydrates. While being mindful of their caloric content, we should be more concerned about their GI. The index is invaluable because it ranks carbohydrates from those that are most healthy to those that are least healthy.

GI Index Table[173]

High Glycemic Foods (60–+)

Dates (dried)	103	Popcorn	72
Parsnips	97	White rice	72
Puffed rice cakes	91	Pineapple	66
Baked potato	85	Beets	64
Pretzels	83	Whole wheat bread	60
Millet	81	Sweet corn	60
French fries	75	Boiled potatoes	60
Bagel	72		

Medium-Glycemic Foods (40–60)

Bananas	58	Green peas	48
Coarse whole grain bread	55	Kiwis	47
Mangos	51	Carrots	47
Brown rice	50	Sweet potatoes	44
Buckwheat	49	Oranges	42
Grapes	49		

Low-Glycemic Foods (Less than 40)

Plums	39	Lentil	29
Navy beans	38	Peaches	28
Pears	38	Barley	22
Yogurt	36	Cherries	22
Apples	34	Cashews	22
Chickpeas	33	Soybeans	18
Skim milk	32	Milk (full fat)	11
Soy milk	30		

In the above table, items with a higher glycemic index rating appear towards the top, that is, they are considered high-glyemic or high in glucose. These sweet products are largely composed of simple molecules that are quickly absorbed into the blood stream. The blood sugar level soars and, if not burnt as energy, they accumulate as fat. If these items are consumed regularly, blood sugar levels may be under ongoing pressure to rise and the body can continuously produce fat. Hence, a high GI is unhealthy for the body.

A diet that has high glycemic levels may suffer adverse effects, such as weight gain and fatigue, as the body struggles to bring down the high blood sugar level. A diet with low glycemic levels includes healthy carbohydrates that break down slowly in the digestive system and provide a steady source of energy. They include a variety of fresh fruits, leafy vegetables, beans, nuts, and legumes. All of them are rich in nutrients.

Another aspect of the GI is the effect certain foods have on triggering insulin, the hormone summoned to regulate sugar level. A rapid rise in blood glucose stimulates the pancreas to release the hormone insulin, which, in turn, lowers the blood glucose. This then stimulates overall appetite, which leads to further eating. Thus, a vicious cycle is produced and the pancreas becomes exhausted, paving the way for the development of diabetes mellitus. It is therefore sensible to eat less refined sugar and more fiber. Such a diet would retard the absorption of glucose and therefore prevent a rapid rise in blood glucose levels.

We would do well to follow the advice of Hippocrates to maintain balance and proportion in the foods we eat. He explained, "There is in man the bitter and the salt, the sweet and the acid, the sour and the insipid, and a multitude of other things, having all sorts of powers both as regards quantity and strength. These, when all mixed and mingled up with one another, are not apparent, neither do they hurt a man; but when any of them is separate, and stands by itself, then it becomes perceptible, and hurts a man."

Good health is hurt when the chemical composition of the body does not function in proper balance and proportion. The secret to health is to consume a well-balanced diet, which sustains the body's normal equilibrium.

Building a robust heart

The human heart outperforms all other hearts in existence, except that of the tortoise, which does not live so intensely. Cardiovascular efficiency provides sustained ability for the heart, lungs, and blood to take oxygen from the air and deliver it throughout the body.

Other benefits of strong cardiovascular performance are a lower blood pressure, a decrease in "bad" cholesterol, and an increase in "good" cholesterol. The body becomes livelier with more energy. Even the mind becomes sharper.

The cardio-respiratory system is the most important component of physical fitness and good health. The system must circulate blood throughout the body. It must supply oxygen and nutrients continuously and remove all waste.

As the body contains only twelve pints of blood, the heart must function efficiently as a pump to circulate the blood. If its efficiency is impaired, a person's energy level drops and he may suffer from constant fatigue.

The circulatory and respiratory systems work together to provide muscles with necessary oxygen. As we breathe, oxygen is picked from the air and carried to the heart. Oxygen is fuel for the body. The more oxygen the muscles receive, the more energetic we become and the better we feel. The heart muscle becomes stronger and works more efficiently.

Since the heart is a muscle, it can be made stronger like any other muscle. Aerobic exercise for thirty minutes at least three times a week enhances cardiac efficiency. Research shows that people who exercise regularly develop extra arteries in the heart muscle. Exercise clears fat from the blood stream, reducing the risk of atherosclerosis.

This fact is comforting to me. It gives me hope that through my own actions I can build a robust heart and achieve good health. Whenever I get the opportunity to swim and run, I feel physically fit.

Your heart may break, but it beats on.

Develop a strong immune system

The human body appears designed for wellness, not illness. Its capacity to ward off infection is astonishing. It is endowed with natural defenses, such as white blood cells that are ever alert to hunt and kill invading viruses and toxic bacteria.

Our immune system serves as a protective shield, both inside and outside the body. The secret to good health lies in tuning up the system to function at its maximum efficiency.

While it is true that genetics affect our lives, we can limit any proneness to illness by leading a healthy lifestyle. Our genetic heritage is like a pack of cards. The hand presented to us may not contain all the aces, but we may play the game with such skill as if we do possess them all. Remarkable are the stories of people who have triumphed over their physical limitations and, with astounding life skills, have gone on to lead long and healthy lives. Renoir suffered arthritis in both hands, yet he was able to paint some of the world's greatest masterpieces. Ludwig van Beethoven was partially deaf in his later years, yet he was able to compose celestial music.

Foremost among these skills is something we discussed a few pages back: eating a well-balanced diet to nourish the body with all the necessary vitamins and minerals. Besides protein, a variety of fresh fruits and vegetables, along with whole grains and nuts, best ensures that the body receives all the essential nutrients. Tests exist to identify nutritional deficiencies.

This diet, in combination with ample sleep, regular exercise, and lots of leisure to relieve stress, helps the body build a powerful immune system.

The benefits of vitamins and minerals

The benefits of vitamins are myriad. They contain numerous enzymes and hormones that keep us alive. They provide the body with energy and help it grow and repair itself. They keep the brain alert and strengthen the bones and the heart muscle. Significantly, they ward off infection and lower the risk of cancer and other diseases.

Vitamin A is a boon to the mind and body. It sharpens vision and helps to prevent night blindness and the formation of cataracts. It has a rejuvenating effect on the skin, making it smooth and supple and defending it against premature aging.

The B Complex vitamins combine as a team to perform a host of amazing functions. They break down carbohydrates, fats, and proteins and convert them into energy. They encourage cells, including nerve cells, to grow and reproduce, while eliminating toxins. B vitamins trigger the production of hormones, enzymes, and red blood cells and the release of folic acid. This substance is responsible for keeping arteries open and thus lessening the chances of a heart attack or stroke. Folic acid also controls a person's mood and appetite.

Vitamin C is indispensable for holding the body together. It makes collagen, a connecting tissue that binds the muscles to the bones and the skeleton together. It heals wounds, cuts, and bruises, lowers blood pressure, and controls cholesterol and blood sugar levels.

Sunshine is an abundant source of Vitamin D. The skin produces vitamin D when exposed to ultraviolet rays from sunlight. Vitamin D helps with the absorption of calcium, which strengthens our bones. More Vitamin D is required in the winter, as there is less sunlight, and as we get older to prevent osteoporosis (thinning of bones).

The single most important factor about Vitamin E is the vital role it plays as an antioxidant in combating free radicals, which we discussed earlier in the section entitled --"Clearing arteries."

Physical injuries are inevitable, and when bleeding occurs, Vitamin K comes to the rescue. It forms clots to stop the bleeding. In addition, it contributes to the building of bones.

Vitamins work best when they are consumed along with minerals. The two groups complement each other in averting and curing ailments and in promoting your body's well being.

Minerals are found in the crust of the earth among layers of rocks. Plants absorb them, so when we feed on plants they enter into our system. Various meats also provide minerals that come from the animals that feed on plants.

Calcium is needed at every age. It keeps the bones young and strong. It is essential to maximize bone mass early in life and minimize thinning of bones later in life.

Chromium intake normalizes blood sugar and cholesterol levels. It also inhibits the clogging of arteries.

Iron provides energy by transporting and storing oxygen in the blood and muscles. It helps to reduce fatigue, improve concentration, and increase resistance to disease.

Magnesium tends to keep blood vessels from constricting. It wards off a rise in blood pressure and thus improves cardiovascular efficiency.

Potassium provides for the smooth functioning of muscles and nerves and reduces cramps. It activates enzymes for energy and stimulates normal movement of the intestinal tract.

Selenium is a powerful detoxifying agent and serves as an antidote to rancid fats. It is also an antioxidant that protects the cell membrane from free radicals.

Zinc is vital for the formation of connective tissues and the health of teeth, bones, nails, hair, and skin. By producing antioxidants and white blood cells, zinc helps the body to resist disease.

A serious deficiency in minerals may undermine health, affect the heart, and raise the risk of cancer. It is important to note that cooking and processing food may reduce the potency of vitamins and minerals.

The chart below lists the various foods that are the source of all minerals. A single *X* indicates this. Some foods score better by providing two or more minerals. A double *X* indicates the foods that contain the most amount of a mineral.

The foods listed in the chart also contain all the vitamins from A to K. It is important that we drink milk and fruit juices and eat a variety of foods to ensure that all the vitamins nourish us. However, a balanced diet alone may not be enough to provide you with all the nutrients. It would be advisable to take vitamin and mineral supplements in consultation with your physician.

Sources of Minerals
Meats and Seafood

	Calcium	Chromium	Iron	Magnesium	Potassium	Selenium	Zinc
Beef,							
Lamb,							
Pork		X	X		X	X	X
Chicken		X	X			X	X
Liver		X	X			X	X
Turkey		X				X	X
Halibut					X	X	X
Mackerel					X	X	X
Oysters		X	X			X	X
Salmon	X					X	X
Sardines	X		X			X	X
Shellfish						X	X
Shrimp/Crab				X		X	X
Tuna			X			X	X

Dairy

	Calcium	Chromium	Iron	Magnesium	Potassium	Selenium	Zinc
Cheese (low fat)	X	X	X	X			
Eggs	X	X					X
Milk	X			X	X		X
Yogurt (low fat)	X			X			X

Grains and Nuts

	Calcium	Chromium	Iron	Magnesium	Potassium	Selenium	Zinc
Almonds	X	X	X	X	X	X	X
Barley, oats, wheat		X	X	X	X	X	X
Bran		X	X				X
Lentils			X	X	X	X	X
Brazil nuts		X		X		X	X
Cashews		X		X			X
Peanuts	X	X	X	X			X
Pecans		X		X			X
Walnuts		X	X	X			X
Flax seed						X	X
Sunflower seeds	X					X	X

Vegetables

	Calcium	Chromium	Iron	Magnesium	Potassium	Selenium	Zinc
Beans	X				X		
Broccoli	X	X	X	X	X		
Brussels sprouts			X				
Cabbage	X						
Chickpeas	X		X	X	X		X
Collards	X						
Corn					X		
Kale	X		X				
Mushrooms		X					
Okra	X			X	X		
Peas		X		X			X
Potatoes	X		X	X			
Soya				X			
Spinach	X		X	X	X		
Sweet Potatoes	X				X		
Turnip	X						

Fruits and Berries

	Calcium	Chromium	Iron	Magnesium	Potassium	Selenium	Zinc
Apricots			X		X		
Avocado					X		
Banana					X		
Cantaloupe					X		
Kiwi					X		
Orange					X		
Prunes			X		X		
Tomato							

Other

	Calcium	Chromium	Iron	Magnesium	Potassium	Selenium	Zinc
Black pepper		X					
Garlic						X	
Tofu	X			X			

IV. A Path to rejuvenation

A natural elixir

Yoga exercises provide a gentle but effective way to promote flexibility among all the joints and other parts of the body. The great thing about yoga is mind-body co-ordination. In practicing the various poses and exercises, visualization is critical. As a yoga specialist said, a person becomes acutely aware of every movement in the exercise from moment to moment. When the mind is focused on every pose and movement, the body itself gets into better shape, and the mind is sharpened too.

We shall discuss briefly seven yoga exercises to promote physical and physiological well-being. The exercises are designed to give us youthful vigor. Repeat each exercise four to six times, which constitutes a set. Progressively increase the number of repeats and sets as you advance in physical fitness.

Gate

1. Exercises all joints of arms and legs; promotes suppleness and elasticity.

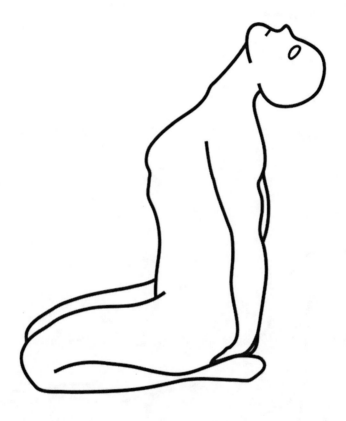

Child

2. Keeps the spine supple; internal organs receive a gentle therapeutic massage.

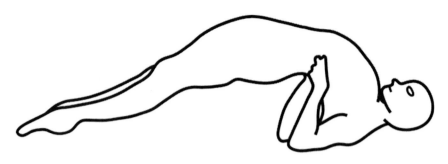

Bridge

3. This posture stimulates the nervous centre of the solar plexus. It reduces tension, improves digestion, and helps eliminate toxins from the abdomen. Good for spine and posture.

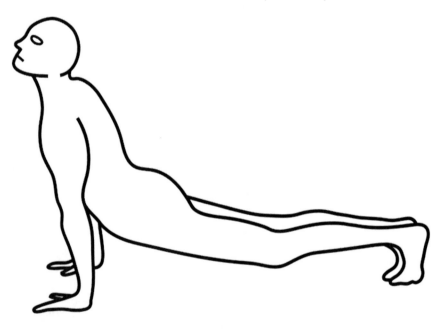

Cobra

4. We are as young as the state of our spine and this exercise strengthens the spine. It averts stooping which may arise at a later age.

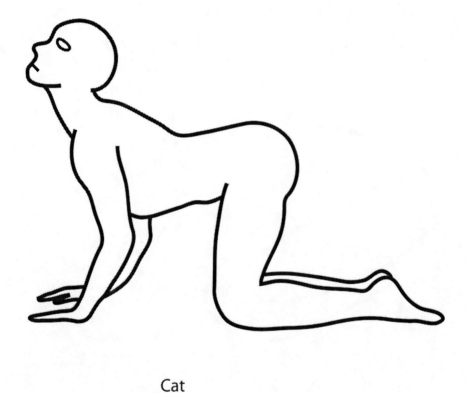

Cat

5. In this exercise, the back is stretched and the arched movement of the body, forward and backward, strengthens the back muscles.

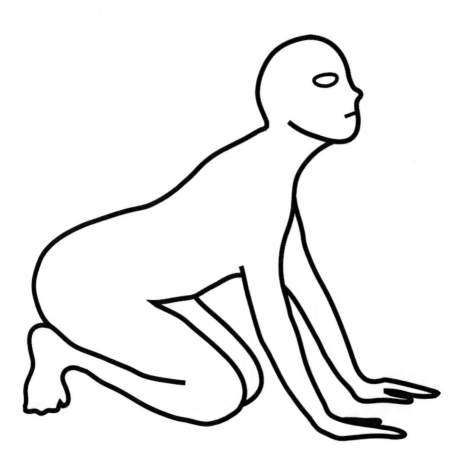

Stretching Dog

6. Helps relieve arithmetic pain and stiffness in shoulders. Relieves fatigue and improves circulation to head and eyes.

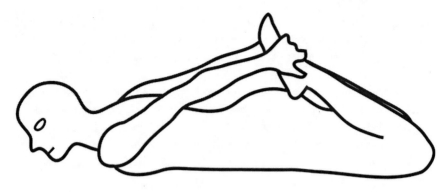

Bow

7. It strengthens back and abdominal muscles. Through a gentle massage it improves the functions of the organs and glands in the kidney and abdominal areas.

Yoga has been practiced in India for more than two thousand years. Yoga distills for us today the wisdom of the ages. This wisdom enlightens us on to how to harmoniously integrate the body with the mind, to attain good health and well-being, and to remain young in spirit.

The above discussion is only a brief introduction to yoga. Those who are seriously interested should take yoga classes.

Suppleness, strength, and stamina

Physical fitness lies in our ability to carry out daily tasks without being overly tired. The body feels young when the limbs and the torso are flexible. Similarly, enhancing the body's strength helps to recapture some of the physical strength of youth. Exercises to increase stamina or endurance endow the body with the physical power of youth.

The combination of these exercises lowers the biological age. Delight yourself in feeling much younger, though your calendar age may be forty or sixty or more.

Suppleness of the body is achieved through yoga or stretching exercises. Through diligent training, people in their seventies and eighties have trained their bodies to acquire the suppleness of those in their twenties or thirties. There is hope for everyone.

Suppleness of the body improves poise and posture and gives it a youthful appearance. You can train your body to move vibrantly like a spring. It can twist and turn sideways, forward and backward, and bend in all directions.

All these movements permit every nerve, tissue, and vein to be replenished with fresh blood and oxygen. Consequently, stiffness of the body, which is caused by stress, is eliminated, and there is a free flow of energy. What results is a feeling of lightness and agility.

Physical strength is an indicator of good health and youthfulness. It refers to the amount of weight one can lift safely. Weight-training exercises make the muscles firmer and larger, and these muscles contribute to greater physical strength. According to a 1990 study published in the *Journal of the American Medical Association*, even among people in their nineties, muscle strength improved significantly after weight training. [174]

Initially, the muscles are invisible, as a layer of fat covers them. Eventually, with diligent weight training and intense physical exercise, the muscles become visible. Stronger muscles also mean leaner muscles, with reduced fat.

The more muscles you have on your frame, the higher is your basic metabolic rate. Expanding muscles reduce fat and eventually narrow your waistline. Since muscles are more dense than fat, your body appears trim, tighter, and more toned. Your face, too, is likely to look radiant.

Stamina, or endurance, is a form of sustained strength. It is a good indicator of health and fitness. Stamina demonstrates how many times one could lift an object or how long one could hold it without fatigue. It is also recommended that exercises should commence with a gentle warm-up and end with a gentle cool down.

Stamina is measured by a person's capacity to sustain his efforts non-stop in cycling, jogging, swimming, or any type of aerobic activity. Brisk walking is as effective as running and rope jumping. All of these exercises provide agility. The primary aim of weight training is to enable the heart and lungs to function efficiently. The bones, ligaments, and skeletal muscles are strengthened, and the body flushes out lactic acid and other toxins.

Progress in weight training is best illustrated in the story of the Greek god Milo. Every day he lifted a small calf. As the calf grew heavier and heavier, Milo's muscles grew stronger and stronger. Eventually, he was able to lift a fully grown cow.

While we improve physically, we also need to grow mentally and spiritually, because growth is evidence of life.

Let centenarians point the way

Lucille Ball said that the secret to stay young is to live honestly, eat slowly, and lie about your age.

On a more serious note, a scientific study of four hundred centenarians in Okinawa, Japan, revealed that they enjoyed near-perfect health throughout their long lives. They had strong bones and low cholesterol levels. Excellent blood pressure contributed to better circulation to the brain, making them more mentally alert for their age. Physical fitness and a healthy lifestyle contributed to their longevity.

Fresh fruit and vegetables were the centrepiece of their diet, amounting to about ten servings a day. They consumed less fat, alcohol, and meat and more fish. Their limited caloric intake was more likely to come from grazing than from gorging.

The lives of centenarians in the Caucasus region of Russia followed a similar pattern. A study by Dan Georagakas, "Learning from the World's Longest Living People," shows that the behavior of centenarians is distinctive for following their own biological rhythms. Average consumption of food is about 1,500–2000 calories a day. These people lead a rugged life, chopping wood, hauling water, and bathing in the mountain streams.

It is, of course, not practical to imitate the lives of such centenarians. We could, however, learn from them to be more leisurely and natural. Centenarians are like old wine; they get better with age. This lifestyle may help us feel young again.

It is wrong to be too romantic about them; like others they do fall sick and suffer injuries. The remarkable thing, however, is their capacity to bounce back to normal health. We, too, can condition ourselves to be resilient.

These centenarians also tell us not to lead a frenzied life because that could shorten our life.

The wonderful world of walking

To stay young we must feel young. Walking provides an excellent way to get and stay in good physical shape. Simple and easy, it is unique because one can walk in a variety of ways: briskly or leisurely, in solitude or with a companion or dog.

The beautiful thing about walking is the opportunity it provides to design your own fitness program. You can walk at your own convenience, at any time, and at any pace or place. It also offers an effective way to achieve cardiovascular efficiency.

A walk in the woods is exhilarating and conducive to a youthful spirit. Admiring green foliage and listening to the sounds of running water and the chirping of birds makes us become one with nature. Add variety to your walk by wading through water, clearing a path through the thicket, or smelling the freshness of the forest air. As you walk, look for Shelley's "sensitive plant that in a garden grew and how the young winds fed it with silver dew."

Living is like walking. Shakespeare said, "Climbing steep hills requires a slow pace at first." Walking uphill might be safer than walking downhill.

We may also note that beyond a rough road there may be a smoother path ahead.

While walking, if possible, chop your own wood, and it will warm you twice.

Besides walking, it requires great art to saunter. Go around old alleys and byways in old neighborhoods looking for old books, old tools, and antiques.

It requires old scissors to cut new silk.

Paradox to ponder
>Nothing is permanent except change.[175]
>--Heraclitus
>
>The time to relax is when you don't have time for it.
>-- Sydney J. Harris.
>
>When I grow old, I want to be like a little boy.[176]
>--Joseph Heller
>
>That man's silence is wonderful to listen to.[177]
>-- Thomas Hardy

153. Laozi, Philip J., *The Daodejing of Laoz* (Hackett Publishing, 2003), p.94.

154. Mencius (c.390–305 BC) was a Chinese philosopher and considered a cofounder of Confucianism. He argued that human beings are naturally good but become corrupted by society.

155. Matthew 19:14, NIV.

156. *The Globe and Mail*, June 18, 2003.

157. Omar Khayyam was an Islamic scholar who was a poet as well as a mathematician. He compiled astronomical tables and contributed to calendar reform and discovered a geometrical method of solving cubic equations by intersecting a parabola with a circle.

158. Ashley Montagu, Growing Young (Greenwood Publishing Group, 1989), 135.

159. Van Gogh was a Dutch post-Impressionist artist. His paintings and drawings include some of the world's best known, most popular, and most expensive pieces.

160. Monet was a founder of French Impressionist painting.

161. Lisa Belkin, *Life's Work: Confessions of an Unbalanced* (Simon & Schuster, 2002),101.

162. Ashley Montagu, Growing Young (Greenwood Publishing Group, 1989).

163. He was a French essayist and had a direct influence on writers the world over, from Shakespeare to Emerson, from Nietzsche to Rousseau.

164. Rhoda Thomas Tripp, *The International Thesaurus of Quotations* (Crowell, 1970), 445.

165. A Spanish novelist, poet, and playwright, de Cervantes was one of the most influential persons in sixteenth-century Spain.

166. Chopra, *Grow Younger, Live Longer.*

167. Excerpta Medica Foundation, *Excerpta Medica* (Excerpta Medica Foundation, 1969), p.355.

168. Smith, *Renewal*, p.6.

169. Ibid.

170. Diogenes Laertius, *The Lives and Opinions of Eminent* (George Bell & Sons, 1895), 231.

171. An ancient Greek physician, Hippocrates is considered one of the most outstanding figures in the history of medicine. He is often referred to as The Father of Medicine.

172. Quoted in *The Globe and Mail*, March 4, 2004, p.A3.

173. Miller, Jennie Brand and Wolever, Thomas. "The New Glucose Revolution," as reprinted in *The Globe and Mail*, March 3, 2004.

174. M. A. Fiatarone, E. C. Marks, N. D. Ryan, C. N. Meredith, L. A. Lipsitz and W. J. Evans, "High-intensity strength training in nonagenarians. Effects on skeletal muscle", *Journal of the American Medical Association*, Vol. 263 No. 22, June 13, 1990.

175. Heraclitus.

176. Joseph Heller, *Something Happened* (Random House Publishing Group, 1975), p.319.

177. Thomas Hardy, *Under the Greenwood Tree* (Penguin Classics, 1998), p.71.

Chapter 5
A Blueprint for Success

Chapter 5
A Blueprint for Success

I. Design a strategy

Success, like beauty, may lie in the eye of the beholder. Bessie Stanley claimed, "He has achieved success who has lived well, laughed often and loved much.."[178] According to N. I. Hamilton, there is "true success when our efforts confer true benefits on others as well as ourselves." William James was interested in achieving enduring success. He stated, "The greatest use of life is to spend it for something that will outlast our life." Temporary gains have their place, but more important are permanent gains that will provide enduring satisfaction.

To get our discussion rolling, we shall accept Christopher Morley's definition of success: "to be able to spend your life in your own way." [179] Morley's definition blends well with Emerson's definition that success lies "in pursuing the best ends through the best means." He also claimed, "High success is likely when we excel in areas that are themselves excellent." Cindy Adams cautions, "Success has made failures of many men."

Attaining success contributes to our happiness, while its lack undermines it. Success shapes our character and gives zest to life, while its lack makes us less energetic and optimistic. So crucial a role does success play in our life that we shall, in this chapter, examine some of its dimensions.

Define your own idea of success

Though we must heed others, ultimately we should know what is best for ourselves. We should be free like the butterflies to do anything that gives us satisfaction provided we do not hurt others. Should we be free to hurt ourselves? A strong case can be made either way. I am of the opinion that we are not free to inflict self-injury. I of course duly respect the reader who may have a contrary opinion.

Success in living may lie in mastering the art of living. While numerous resources exist on how to master many art forms, not much is available on how to excel in the art of living. Ultimately, our personal experiences and our own inner strength are a useful guide to living. One supreme skill to acquire is the art of avoiding pain.

Life is a success not only in accomplishing great things but in also doing little things, like stirring a child's mind by answering her questions. This gives us tremendous satisfaction. The more we define success clearly, the more likely we are to achieve it. To attain this objective, experts recommend the following three steps: form a clear vision, establish specific goals, and write a mission statement.

1. Form a clear vision.

Vision is a part of wisdom. Jonathan Swift[180] (1667–1745) described it as the art of seeing the invisible. Dr. Martin Luther King Jr. eloquently expressed an example of vision in his famous speech, "I have a dream." He expressed the hope that "one day … the sons of former slaves and the sons of former slave owners will be able to sit down together at the table of brotherhood."[181] To be resourceful we must have a dream. Such a vision gives us the capacity to see the long-term picture and provides a purpose and focus to life.

Our vision is like a pilot's flight chart. We must know where we are going before we take off. From a wide range of options, we learn to navigate a course of action in line with our plans and destination. The vision enables us to see clearly not only the things that are good for ourselves but also what's good for others.

Adding to our clarity is a thought-out value system. To what degree are we materialistic and altruistic, and what is the correct mix of these two values? During the next decade, should we bend our energies primarily in making money or in doing humanitarian work? How can we advance our individual interests while being mindful of the interests of others? And how can we get the most out of life while containing our aggressive instincts? In answering these questions, we would have clarity in our minds about our view of success.

If we are politically minded, we should think more about the next generation than about the next election. If we are ecologically minded, we should work for a habitat that is green and pleasant. Our vision is sharpened when we have a strong motive, a cause, a creed, a passion, and as John Masefield[182] (1878–1967) said, "a star to steer by." This vision helps us on the road to success and also provides us with *flashes of wisdom and moments of delight*.

2. Establish specific goals.

While a vision provides us with a direction for our destination, our goals show us the footprints and the mileposts. Our goals refer to specific objectives that we set for ourselves in a career, finances, family, and friends. They may be set yearly, monthly, or even weekly. The best goals are those that are precise and well defined. Overwhelming changes are inevitable. In anticipation of change, we should have plans to review and modify our goals both for the short and long terms. Goals carved in stone are prone to failure. Leaving a contingency for the unexpected is prudent. Thus, the baby we hoped for may not arrive and the promotion pined for may not arise. Goals have a tendency to slip away, and we may have to take a detour to regain them.

Setting realistic goals is a challenging task. Chances are greater of achieving excellence in one sport rather than in two, or of securing the loyalty of the membership rather than winning their affection.

Albert Einstein presented three suggestions on how to clearly entwine vision with goals. First, he said that we could find simplicity out of clutter. Second, from discord make harmony. And finally, seek opportunity in the midst of difficulty. We may conclude this section with Henry David Thoreau's hopeful advice that "men are born to succeed, not to fail."

3. Write a mission statement.

The vision and the goals can be embodied in a single document called a mission statement. Stephen R. Covey, in his international bestseller *The Seven Habits of Highly Effective People,* suggests that a mission statement addressed to oneself "serves as a point of reference to our daily strivings."[183] He poses the question whether the things we do have any bearing on our ultimate aims in life, or are we straying away from our main missions? Here are examples of a mission statement that have been inspired by the major contents of my book.

We suggest from Chapter 1: Your vision in life may be to "enjoy inner peace and calm." It may include a search for inner harmony, inner contentment, and a desire to practice magnanimity and lead a serene life.

If you wish, you may also include in your mission statement from Chapters 2–4, a desire to "give yourself a dazzling mind" and "be ever young in spirit."

The desire for success that we are now discussing could itself be a part of the mission statement. We may also include a reference to seeking "abundant energy in everyday life," which we shall discuss in our final chapter.

Let us consider some practical goals that we can pursued every day.

- Admire at least one painting, read at least one inspiring passage, and listen to some soothing music.
- Perform a kind act to at least one person outside your family.
- Engage in about twenty minutes of meditation in the morning and evening.
- Feel fit and add suppleness to your body by performing the Sun Salutation yoga exercise for at least three minutes.

- In an open space, engage in some deep breathing to feel relaxed.
- Interact with one or more persons with whom you can have a conversation that is pleasant, stimulating, and full of laughter.
- Develop one new proficiency a year.

As short-term and long-term goals often overlap, they may be blended and pursued together. Thus, we may set target dates for advancement in our career, in the near or distant future. With regard to health, we may set targets for achieving optimal physical fitness, as we discussed in Chapter 4.

The future comes one day at a time. A good way to prepare for the future is to consider each day as a new day, offering a new beginning and a new opportunity.

II. Engage in quantum thinking

When we dare more, we achieve more success. A ship is safe in the harbor, but it is meant for the high seas. Absolute safety is unproductive.

Fortune favors the audacious. Most of the time we must be content in making progress that is only incremental. Occasionally, however, opportunities may arise when our progress is phenomenal. Sometimes, this happens when our mind looks at things in an unusual or unconventional manner.

Consequently, the mind becomes imaginative and is able to move forward in quantum leaps. A simple example illustrates the point: How do you turn a 9 into a 6 with only one change? Thinking afresh, all that you do is add the letter S, in the following manner:

IX
SIX

A seemingly impossible task becomes possible if we think about it in an unusual way. How do you cut a cake into eight equal slices with only three strokes with a knife?

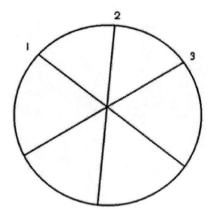

Three strokes with the knife, but only six pieces of cake.

Looking at the cake in only two dimensions will certainly yield no results. In the diagram above we have tried to slice the cake with three strokes, but this yielded six pieces. Is it possible to divide the cake into eight slices with only three strokes? Consider the cake in three dimensions, and you'll find an easy solution. First, cut the cake from top to bottom into two equal slices. Next, cut the cake again from top to bottom into four equal slices. Finally, cut the cake through the side into eight equal slices.

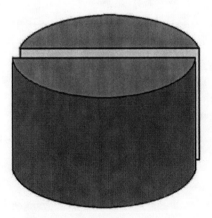

First, cut top to bottom, making two pieces.

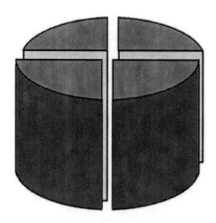

Cut again top to bottom, making four pieces.

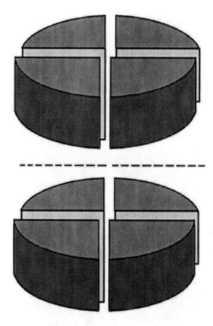

Finally, cut through the side of the cake, making eight pieces.

Those who engage in quantum thinking are more likely to achieve high success. They love to experiment, discover, and innovate in ways that bring them revolutionary results. A historical example is Galileo[184] (1564–1642), whose telescopic observations confirmed Copernicus' theory that the Earth moves around the sun. This discovery shook the contemporary world and provided a basis for the development of modern science.

In our own day, through international cooperation, quantum thinking has produced spectacular success. The microchip has changed the world, and miracle rice has helped feed the world. The splitting of the atom has released atomic energy, and the mapping of DNA has opened new frontiers in medicine and genetics. Quantum thinking involves taking a large leap forward, when a well nigh impossibility becomes a possibility.

Cultivate a fertile imagination

Wisdom lies not only in seeing, but also in foreseeing.

What is now proved was at one time only imagined. A good example is the design of an aircraft in the sixteenth century by Leonardo DaVinci. His experience tells us that we are not to assume that what is now unknown is forever unknowable.

Imagination is more important than knowledge. It helps us to look at the mundane world with a pair of fresh eyes. It is the source of creative ideas and new perspectives. It enables us to see the invisible, such as the wind that moves the sails and the hidden qualities of people. It is fascinating, for instance, to observe an eminent surgeon possess the heart of a lion, the eye of an eagle, and the gentleness of a deer.

Imagination is essential for success. Writing interesting letters, prudently managing time, and getting along well with those above and below us in social status calls for imagination. It is the eye of the soul because it brightens the things we touch and enhances the quality of our thoughts.

One way to sharpen our imagination is to look upon the truth as a contradiction. By looking for the opposite characteristics of a person, we can gather exciting new insights. It would be normal to consider human behavior as good or bad, beautiful or ugly. But this is an oversimplification. A little reflection reveals that these concepts are relative. It is possible for one to be good *and* bad, beautiful *and* ugly, but under different circumstances.

Thus, what is good for hunger is bad for fever, and what is beautiful in ballet looks ugly in wrestling. Everything is good and beautiful for whatever purpose it serves well, but bad and ugly for whatever it does not serve.

A conventional view is to regard poison as dangerous because it kills. A bold and different perspective shows that a miniscule amount of it, treated with extreme caution, is beneficial. Toxin from the toadfish, for instance, has been used to assist brain surgery. Venom from the cobra has been extracted to form an antidote to treat cobra strikes.

Imitating opposite features in nature sharpens the imagination. Roses are symbolic of elegance, but their fairness fades fast. More important, they are inseparable from the thorns, and in smelling these roses we cannot avoid being pricked. Similarly, our joys are likely to be interwoven with sorrows. Obstacles are inevitable.

Nature also shows us that when old life fades away, new life emerges. Decaying plants are surrounded by new shoots displaying new life. What is relevant for success is the importance of discarding outdated ideas and embracing innovative ideas.

Seek not a larger garden but finer seeds[185]

Philip fancied himself to be a gardener like Adam in the Garden of Eden. He toiled long and hard, but the yield was disappointing. Poor Philip was locked into an old paradigm. He believed firmly that more tilling and fertilizing would turn the soil around and produce a rich harvest. Then one day, while taking a walk in the garden, he was inspired to engage in quantum thinking. A simple idea dawned on him to produce better results. Why not sow finer seeds of tomatoes and cucumber, celery, mace, and thyme? Philip watched in amazement the luxuriant growth, and he reaped a rich harvest of fruits and vegetables. He wondered how a small change in his thinking could produce such wondrous results.

On a more modest scale, quantum thinking has been the principal force for success in product innovation. How significantly the quality of life has improved for people with the arrival of the digital camera, the palm computer, and various household appliances.

Taste the ocean in one sip

The ocean is vast, but its salty nature can be tasted in one sip. Similarly, knowledge is vast; a whole lifetime is not enough to understand even a fraction of reality. Through quantum thinking, however, we can uncover the wrappings and reach for the gem of truth. As in the case of the oyster, we can overlook the shell of polemics and discover the pearl of pure knowledge.

Getting to the essence of things is a fruitful way to acquire deep knowledge and achieve personal advancement, which is a key to personal success. Thanks to the strategy of quantum thinking, *it is possible to achieve more through less effort.*

An example of quantum thinking is to delve into children's encyclopaedias. They are a rich source of knowledge, presented in an easy to understand manner. Eminent writers love to write for children and have a remarkable ability to break through complexity and present the essence of things in a simplified manner. Their writings would be a boon to adults. Whether it's the origin of religion or human evolution, the laws of nature or the theory of relativity, a simplified version of each concept is readily available.

"Find the sweetest essences in the smallest glasses"

The above quotation from Emily Dickinson[186] (1830–1886) offers a good idea of how to engage in quantum thinking. Vincent and Viola were studious, but their grades were average. In frustration, they turned to Felix, who earned high grades while having lots of fun. He advised them to modify their method of study; instead of consulting the text repeatedly, he suggested they write a comprehensive summary. Further, he urged them to give careful thought to a summary of the summaries in about five pages. He then asked them to constantly review and refine this document so that it would critically reflect the text.

The document was well designed, with all the points arranged sequentially. Concepts were represented by only one letter, such as A and E, to represent *anima* and *electra*. Many arrows in all directions showed their interrelationships.

Vincent and Viola considered the document to be precious, and their grades improved significantly. They were successfully engaged in quantum thinking. The five pages were like five small glasses that contained the essence of their subject matter. They sipped from them frequently, which also gave them *flashes of wisdom and moments of delight*.

Untying the Gordian Knot

According to Greek legend, Gordius came to the town of Phrygia in an oxcart, and soon the townsmen crowned him king. In gratitude, Gordius dedicated his oxcart to Zeus and tied it to a pole with an intricate knot. People were fascinated by it for the challenge it posed to untie it, and they named it the Gordian Knot. They hassled at length how to untie it, all to no avail. The legend grew that whoever was able to untie it would rule all of Asia. Then one day Alexander the Great walked by. True to his reputation as a brilliant strategist, he acted decisively. He called for a sword and cut the knot to the astonishment of all.

The story of the Gordian Knot illustrates the point about the need to act quickly and decisively in difficult situations.

In life there are often simple solutions to complex problems.

An unconventional view of success

We saw earlier that Christopher Morley's idea of success was "to be able to spend your life in your own way."

This is a distinctive view of success, and we shall examine this view from many dimensions. Thus, we would do well to spend a day with the sight and sound of beauty, the contemplation of mystery, and the search for truth and perfection.

According to the Upanishads, part of the ancient Hindu scriptures, truth is like honey. It is sweet and constitutes one compound, though the nectar is gathered from many flowers. Similarly, the truth is one, though its origin is traced to many sources.

In the midst of a busy life, we must take a little time to reflect on nature and admire its beauty and mystery. How exhilarating it is to hear the sound of rolling waters, to smell the freshness of the air after the rain, and observe how the beautiful flowers accept the visit of honeybees.

Another unconventional view of success is to realize that our finest hours are spent not among large crowds but in conversing with a few select people. We may also read great books, listen to enchanting music, wander in a forest of pine trees, and peer into the microscope to unravel the secrets of nature.

III. Be creative

Creating is the true essence of life.
— Reinhold Niebuhr[187] (1892–1971)

To be creative is a sign of success, a mark of progress, and an expression of fulfilment. It is a process of bringing forth something new, producing something that is both useful and enjoyable. A creative act need not be a masterpiece. It could be the design of a lovely dress or the delivery of a fine speech.

Anyone can be creative and so be successful. This point is well illustrated in the story of a ten-year-old boy who found his brother's hand trapped under a machine. He acted decisively by using a piece of hardwood as a lever to lift the machine, which was heavier than he was, and thus rescue the crushed hand. His heroic act displayed quick thinking and finesse under intense pressure. The accident demonstrated how a crisis triggered his potential to shine.

Everyone has hidden potential and has an aptitude to do well in at least one field or endeavor. It could be in art, acting, or accounting, or music, mechanics, or mathematics. Social skills like organizing, networking, and cooperating are another field. Personal acts of kindness, love, and empathy win appreciation.

To be creative is to be natural, with the spontaneous urge to develop and to unfold.

Here are some conditions that contribute to success through creative thinking.

Aiming for achievement
Nothing great is created suddenly, any more than a bunch of grapes.

Many great ideas have been conceived before, but to profit from them we must mull over them again to let them sink into our mind. The ideas of great writers are a case in point.

To Freud, human sexuality is a key to understanding human behaviour. To Marx[188] (1818–1883), the acquisition of wealth is the main focus of man. T. S. Eliot wrote, "Half of the harm that is done in this world is due to people who want to feel important. They don't mean to do harm. But the harm does not interest them." To Alfred Adler[189] (1870–1937), deep insights about man can be gleaned from his constant struggle for achievement.

Adler claims that each person is born into a world with a sense of inferiority. We start as weak, helpless children and strive to overcome these deficiencies by trying to be superior to those around us. He called this struggle a striving for superiority, and it is a powerful motivating factor behind all human thoughts, emotions, and behaviors.

Today, accomplished artists and writers, powerful business people, and aspiring politicians have a compelling need to excel. Initially, they experience feelings of inferiority, which they attempt to overcome by shining in their respective fields. Many are satisfied, but others are not. Their quest proceeds in a continuous spiral, such as an Olympic gold medalist who still yearns for more medals.

Adler was also concerned about individuals at the other end who find life to be unfair. They have had more than their due share of disappointments, and success remains elusive. Here again we cite the Differential Principle. The negative feelings that people hold vary in degree and intensity. Many are troubled only marginally, while others are overwhelmed. When this happens they may slip into a state described by Adler as an inferiority complex.

How do we get rid of our negative feelings? A first step is to change our attitude. We should never give up hope, because as long as there is life there is hope. To observe amputees facing life is a lesson in inspiration, for instance. We should not feel helpless, because we are not as helpless as we think. Surely, there are a few good things going for us.

We can overcome feelings of inferiority by building self-confidence and self-esteem. Just as a bird builds a nest one twig at a time, our little acts of kindness and our little achievements over time have a cumulative effect. Eventually we are proud of having built our own nest of accomplishment.

Fine-tuning our judgment

A children's poem states that things are not what they seem; for example, skim milk might appear as cream to a child. We know that a straight stick appears crooked in the water. This is only an optical illusion caused by the refraction of light. The stars appear close together, but some of them are millions of light years apart. Often the winner in a race is determined solely by a photo taken by a high-speed camera.

Innocent people have been convicted on apparently plausible evidence, but with the emergence of modern DNA technology, some of these convictions have been overturned.

Some aspects of reality have hidden dimensions. This is illustrated in the example of an ant moving on a drinking straw.[190]

From a distance, on one dimension it appears as if the ant is moving either forward or backward on the straw. But the appearance is not real if we take a closer look at the straw from another dimension. The straw is circular and the ant is able to move in a circular way.

For our conclusions to be valid, we must look beyond initial appearances and search for fresh and sound evidence to fine-tune our judgment.

Building self-confidence

We saw in Chapter 2 that self-esteem is a mark of a healthy personality. A "sister" concept is self-confidence, which is a basis for achievement. It can be defined as a capacity to have a positive and realistic view of oneself. It is characterized by optimism, eagerness, enterprise, pride, affection, independence, and trust. It includes emotional maturity and an ability to handle criticism. A spontaneous burst of energy seems to flow through a self-confident person, making him unafraid of facing challenges.

A lack of self-confidence may lead to self-doubt, isolation, overconformity, distrust, and even depression. It arises from negative life experiences at home or work and being obsessed with disappointments, which are treated as failures instead of learning experiences.

Self-confidence has to be built gradually, each advance serving as a stepping-stone for further advances. For example, practicing before a small audience and then moving on to address larger audiences eliminates the fright of public speaking. Even the great Winston Churchill was nervous when he first spoke in Parliament, but he later became one of Britain's greatest orators.

Marie Curie insisted that we have confidence in ourselves that we are gifted for something, which we must at whatever cost try to attain.

It is not possible to be self-confident in all fields. Even outstanding personages could be very ordinary outside their field of expertise.

A practical way to acquire self-confidence is to picture yourself vividly as a winner and as a success. Over time this image may become a part of your personality.

An attitude to avoid is overconfidence, which is caused by a high ego. A politician who underestimates his opponents may come to grief, and a sports team that basks in its superiority may get soundly beaten.

Self-reliance is a foundation for self-confidence. It can be built gradually, by laying one stone at a time. Through self-reliance we learn to use our inner resources to a greater extent to face the challenges of life. It is cultivated in numerous ways. By interacting with people one person at a time, we may gather invaluable trust and experience. Our friends and associates provide us ample opportunities to perfect our skills in communication, initiative, and intuition. As our relationships become smoother, our self-confidence becomes greater.

We become more self-reliant by being more resourceful. And our capacity to be resourceful in befriending people is limitless. Forming new acquaintances and renewing old acquaintances, provoking laughter and sharing of grief, could produce a triple effect: our inner strength increases, our self-esteem rises, and our self-confidence improves.

A lack of self-confidence is not necessarily related to lack of ability. Instead, it arises from focusing too much on the unrealistic expectations of society.

A concept associated with self-confidence is self-respect. It is the "noblest garment with which a man may clothe himself," said Samuel Johnson. It is the cornerstone of our dignity because it helps us to earn the respect of others.

An aid to self-confidence is self-control. It gives a person much advantage over another, enabling him to remain calm and unruffled under difficult circumstances. Ralph Waldo Emerson wrote that when you keep cool, you command everybody.

Aim for perfection, but be not a perfectionist

Pure water contains no fish.

While it is a worthy aim to seek perfection, we cannot do so in all our endeavors. We have to be very selective in which areas we wish to be perfect. In the field of gymnastics, for instance, it is possible to win a perfect score.

In the exact sciences like physics or mathematics, it is within our reach to obtain a perfect grade. At the sophisticated level, the conductor of an orchestra directs the symphony to perfection.

To strive for perfection in all our endeavors is impossible. Life is too complex and human behavior too unpredictable for us to arrange our affairs to perfection. Many individuals do achieve perfection in some fields, but fall short in other fields. Consequently, they are frustrated and may even make their associates feel frustrated. A perfectionist attitude is illustrated in the behavior of Harold. He earns 92 percent in an exam but is miserable in comparison to Harriet, who rejoices with a mark of 88 percent. What was important to her was to experience pride and joy in a good performance and not be obsessed about an ideal mark.

Steven J. Hendlin has defined a perfectionist as "someone who thinks that anything short of perfection in performance is unacceptable."[191] The perfectionist is seldom satisfied because he always feels that he could have done better. He emphasizes the negative and not the positive.

Prudence demands that we seek perfection only in areas where it is practical, like composing a brilliant speech. In other areas we must rest content with our best endeavors. It is also prudent to realize that losses are bound to happen and we must learn to cope with them, gracefully. Last, it is wise to appreciate much of what is good in people and learn to tolerate their imperfections, just as we expect them to tolerate ours. It is vital to cultivate a fine understanding with those with whom we interact significantly.

Human relations is one area in which we can never have perfect understanding. Even among lovers, misunderstandings arise because, as we saw in Chapter 3, no two individuals perceive the same thing in the same way. As all human beings are imperfect, it is unrealistic to expect perfection from anyone. To aim for perfection and not be a perfectionist is to adopt a balanced approach to life, which is very rewarding.

It is wise to realize that perfect order, perfect justice, and perfect harmony are never found in this world. It is, however, very practical to pursue excellence. As we realize that we are what we repeatedly do, the search for excellence becomes a real habit, which is a happy state to be in.

The riches of peak experiences

Realistically, we cannot always be at our best. There are times when we are in danger of spreading ourselves too thin.

Our life resembles nature. Just as every hill has a valley and every crest has an ebb, our life follows certain rhythms of highs and lows, ups and downs. To be in tune with this rhythm is a mark of wisdom.

Peak experiences may happen when we transform a breakdown into a breakthrough, or a lemon into lemonade. Such experiences may enable us to think more clearly and feel more deeply. As a result, we may excel in new ways, be more relaxed, and feel more exuberant.

We may tweak our peak experiences by asking ourselves what is it that we most like to listen to, to look at, to smell, to touch, and to do. Music is a universal language and is one of the most inspiring stimuli for many people. Painting works wonders as well. It turns dull moments into pleasant moments. Like painters of all ages, we can count on nature as an abundant source of imagination. Capturing the marvelous designs of nature, such as the beautiful design of a blue star sapphire, fills our soul with delight.

Engaging in intellectual and emotional intimacies, as we saw in Chapter 3, provokes creative ideas, and so do spirited discussions with friends and associates. Walking in the woods or by the ocean stirs our peak experiences. When they do occur, it is important that we savor them and are not drawn away by distractions. Peak experiences lead to creative thinking, which again provides us with *flashes of wisdom and moments of delight*.

The benefits of visualization

Many successful people have attributed their achievements to the power of visualization, the capacity to form mental images. With regard to health, for instance, a woman could visualize herself as sound and healthy, filled with vitality and energy. It's little wonder that visualization has been widely practiced in areas such as sports, business, the arts, and entertainment.

Practiced regularly, mental rehearsals improve performances. Psychologically, it has been demonstrated that mental imagery is very similar to actual imagery. Consequently, forming positive mental images is indispensable for laying the foundation for achieving excellence. Tom Kubistant, in his work *Performing Your Best*, provides examples of illustrious sport figures who reached the pinnacles of excellence through visualization.

Phil Mahre, the ski champion, rehearsed twenty times before the final event. During the rehearsal, he would go through vividly and in great detail his journey through the entire course. In his mind, he drew pictures of navigating smoothly past every tree and turn. In the finals, he skied almost perfectly; that brought him victory and glory.

Golfer Jack Nicklaus has talked about how he mentally rehearsed all the shots for all eighteen holes.

High jump champion Dwight Stones mentally pictured himself several times gracefully flying over the bar. The final jump was actually carried out with exquisite skill.

Visualization plays a pivotal role in dancing. Dancers frequently choreograph themselves to move with detailed elegance. They may imagine themselves to be a swan or an impala, able to move with grace and poise. In this way dancers reach excellence.

Visualization is highly popular and effective in business circles, too, especially amongs salespeople. Managers and entrepreneurs also have found mental rehearsals to be an effective tool in the preparation of speeches and presentations.

IV. Nature's guide to success

A single flower envies not the many thorns.
—Rabindranath Tagore[192] (1861–1941)

This quotation from the Indian poet Tagore provides a beautiful example of how it can be natural to be unique. The flower stands alone gracefully, unafraid of its many hostile neighbors. Similarly, we must maintain our uniqueness, unafraid of the opinions of cynics and critics. Goethe referred to such people as those who are impossible to please because they are never pleased with themselves.

In this world there is no other person who is exactly like you. You have your own unique background, experiences, values, and way of thinking. It is our own uniqueness that provides us ample raw materials to engage in creative thinking. As Denis Diderot, the French painter, wrote in a typical artistic style, "We must find our own true perch in this world." To take another example from nature, eagles fly alone, but sheep flock together.

Our travel experiences are a rich source for creative imaginations. The Chinese amaze us with their large mobile flower gardens. A range of plants bearing a variety of flowers are grown in green covered pots. The garden looks very natural, as if the plants are rising from the ground. The pots are arranged in a beautiful floral design, with the flowers fluttering in the breeze. The garden becomes "mobile" when the pots are constantly relocated and rearranged to display elegant floral designs.

Soar like the geese in graceful flight

To observe a flock of geese in flight is a beautiful sight—how well they fly in a V formation led by a head bird. In flight they support each other and display excellent teamwork when they take turns to assume the lead position. Thus, when the head bird retreats, the one immediately behind assumes the leadership. Together they fly at a faster speed than those who choose to fly solo. When one falls behind, the goose tries to return to the flock and is readily accepted.

This interesting behavior of geese illustrates that salient qualities of success have a certain basis in nature.

Naturalists explain that the forces at work in nature are of much relevance in understanding the conditions that lead to human success and failure. Birds are endowed with a great capacity to adjust to the changing winds . This quality is dependent, however, on their communication with each other. Counting on their common momentum, they go through turbulence yet retain a clear sense of direction. They are willing to accept the leadership of the head bird and change course if necessary. Most important, there is a sense of "equity" in sharing the burden of leadership.

This example illustrates that our very survival depends on pursuing common interests through cooperation. If we opt to be loners, we do so at our own peril. Very quickly we must accept our folly and humbly seek reintegration to lead a full life.

Following the universal law of adaptation

Adaptation is a universal law of nature. All plants and animals must accept it to survive and live successfully. From insects to fish, birds to mammals, all forms of life must either adapt or perish. It is amazing how organisms win the battle to live through successful adaptation.

While bears hibernate to escape the winter, the arctic tern flies from pole to pole. Camels in the desert go for days without water. The salamander is a primitive organism. When a part of its limb is severed, the remaining part regenerates to grow a new limb. The extraordinary adaptation of these creatures stems from their powerful urge to live.

The capacity of human beings to adapt determines their capacity to succeed in living. The behavior of Inuit people in the arctic and the Kalahari Bushmen in the desert offers studies in contrast. It is a tribute to the human spirit to see how well they adapt to the opposite extremes of two harsh environments.

American and Canadian history offers copious examples of how people from all over the world adapted remarkably to this continent, built successful lives, and made fortunes. Adaptation is a path to success, because beneath the challenges lie hidden opportunities.

Forming a fine temperament

Few guarantees exist in life, but one that comes close is the ability to acquire a mastery over anger. Controlling it empowers the mind to think clearly, plan calmly, and act prudently. It finesses our judgement, smoothes relationships, and earns the respect of others. A fine temperament is an invaluable asset.

A proneness to anger is a liability. It is a barrier to success because it impairs the power to reason and undermines our relationships, particularly within the family and at work. Anger is costly, because it dissipates energy, lessens our control over life, and can even be deadly. The ancient Greeks wrote that against anger even the gods struggle in vain. In modern times, anger and rage may cause you to age.

Anger is a universal negative emotion. It is inevitable as it arises from the frustrations of life, such as traffic jams and long lines. People express it in various degrees, ranging from minimal anger to anger that is pent-up, protracted, and waiting to explode.

Anger is a natural human phenomenon. It is an extreme reaction to provoking life situations. A mature person knows not to be too perturbed by them. Thus, if someone insults you as a "waffler," call him a pancake and diffuse your anger.

The chances of attaining success in life are enhanced when reason reigns over passion, as we discussed in Chapter 1. As uncontrollable anger hinders success, it is important to examine the causes of anger and learn how to address them.

Robert Allan and Donna Blass, in *Getting Control of Your Anger,* argue that anger often arises through sheer frustration when our needs and wants remain unfulfilled. Like fear and pain, it is a warning signal to initiate action to satisfy our requirements. These requirements include a desire to lead a comfortable life, the need for affection and security, and the opportunity to develop our potential. When threatened with impediments to satisfy these needs, a normal human reaction is to get angry. We ask, why are things stacked against us, and why are we losing control?

Obviously, anger is a purely emotional response and does not solve anything, except to alert you. To diffuse the anger we must identify the needs, minimize frustrations, and take constructive measures to satisfy the needs. If one's security is threatened by a single act of infidelity, for instance, anger is a natural reaction. Forgiveness, however, has a therapeutic effect if the offending party is contrite.

A sober and rational approach to life, with a high tolerance for frustration, is more likely to ensure success in our endeavors. Allan and Blass assert that the principal cause for anger is a perception of injustice. The behavior of people is sometime obnoxious. They could be mean, selfish, disrespectful, or disparaging. In spite of their provocations, we must learn to temper our feelings and not boil with anger.

A sense of humor turns tables and makes us feel good. With a group of authors, Alfred was humiliated with the comment that he was an obscure writer. Alfred, however, had the last laugh when he replied that peacocks do not win prizes at poultry shows. In another example, Feronia challenged Frederick to a debate. Aiming to put her down, Frederick said that he debated only with equals. Feronia remained calm at the insult and gently said, "Why don't you debate someone superior?" to the applause of all. In these two cases, a sense of wit turned angry situations into funny episodes.

A major challenge facing each of us is how to control anger when subject to grave provocation, such as the treachery of people. Building a fine temperament is good armor against any provocation, including road rage. The elements of a fine temperament lie in approaching life's provocations in a calm and mature manner. It is vital to initiate action in measured steps while refraining from any form of revenge.

A healthy approach to a treacherous act may lie in a firm resolve never to be naïve or gullible, to rely less on unfamiliar people, and count more on familiar and trustworthy people.

Developing a fine temperament is like cultivating a taste for fine music. As Pat Conroy says, "Without music, life is a journey through a desert."[193] The music enriches our leisure activities, which cushion us against the irritants of a competitive life. The lyrics help us to enjoy nature, unperturbed by the many annoyances that come our way. Music helps us to calm down and not overreact to the pressures of life. Sharing musical appreciation while engaging in a spirited conversation with family and friends fills the heart with gladness that ill will is banished and goodwill prevails.

A fine temperament is built with greater mind-body coordination. Stimulating the mind and exercising the body promotes mental and physical fitness. We saw in Chapter 1 we need "something to live for." And we saw in Chapter 4 the need to improve our suppleness, strength, and stamina.

Inspiring the mind with great ideas leaves little room for minor nuisances, which needlessly bother us. If we are concerned about the chances of success, we must remember that no noble task was ever achieved without some risk. We should also cultivate a breadth of understanding, which brings the distant nearer and makes the stranger a brother.

And when we experience unkind acts, we may neutralize them with kind acts, which serve like a balm. A smile, a hug, and a heartfelt compliment put us in a pleasant mood, as we saw in Chapter 1.

There are several paths to success, and while a few are smooth, many are rough. While we seek the smooth highways of life, we should never be afraid to tackle the rough and bumpy paths to our destination.

V. Sustaining success

If you can think of yesterday without regret and of tomorrow without fear, you are on the road to success. Pursuing these twin goals provides us a mental tonic that enables us to wake up in the morning and look forward to the day.

Life is a paradox and so is success. Just as we can win the battles and lose the war, we can achieve great success but pay a great price. It is therefore essential to seek success in a balanced and thoughtful way to avoid costly consequences.

We need to realize that both success and failure are often the result of accidents. Therefore, we should base our success not too much on luck but on sound preparation.

Turn stumbling blocks into stepping-stones

"A block of granite," Thomas Carlyle wrote, "which was an obstacle in the path way of the weak, becomes a stepping stone in the path way of the strong."

Truth is often a contradiction. Shelley believed that the sweetest melodies arise from the saddest songs. *Wei ji* or *wei xi* is the Chinese word that denotes both crisis and opportunity. In life, opportunity may come disguised as problems, and out of the depths of failure may arise chances of success.

Sometimes, a breakdown could lead to a breakthrough. If a tree dies, plant another in its place.

The fear of failure is a stumbling block; overcoming it is a stepping-stone to success. The life of Abraham Lincoln well illustrates this point. He suffered repeated failures, which only increased his determination to use them as springboards to success. His business ventures were a disaster, and so were his quests for public office. He suffered immensely from a wife who tormented him constantly, and he was not considered good-looking. Yet, this man was to become one of America's greatest presidents. What we can best learn from him is his incomparable tenacity.

When I visited the Lincoln Memorial in Springfield, Illinois, Lincoln seemed to come alive. We could learn from the life of Lincoln not to let the fear of failure stifle our search for success. Overcoming this fear is possible by first realizing that it is often exaggerated. Facing the sources of fear enables us to combat the many uncertainties of life. Fear of the unknown and fear of strangers are perhaps two of the most common fears. It is said that nothing in life is certain except death and taxes. In fact, the only certainty is uncertainty. Wisdom therefore tells us that, uninhibited by fear, we should vigorously pursue our ends if our chances of success are fair. To slip into inaction due to fear of failure is folly.

But we should not attempt the impossible. We cannot turn a raven into a falcon.

Many people are fearful of success that comes with high stress. They are not competitive and prefer a simple life. Thus, they may forego advancement in their career to avoid the strain of added responsibilities.

For non-competitive people, being involved in what they consider to be a rat race is a stumbling block to true success. They would appreciate inner peace and calm as a stepping-stone to success. Maybe in this way they may also enjoy *flashes of wisdom and moments of delight.*

Getting unstuck

"No matter how rich, powerful, successful, or admired you are, you can take a wrong turn, lose your way, skid off the road, and find yourself knee deep in quicksand and sinking fast. At least once in a lifetime, and more likely, many times, you and I may get stuck."[194]

Getting stuck is like the wheels of your car spinning in the mud or seeing few alternatives to our current problems. At its worst, being stuck means feeling fully trapped in a situation that seems totally out of control.

How do we get unstuck? First and foremost, our attitude must change. If we treat life like a journey, we must be prepared to take detours to bypass barriers. We have to put up with delays and drive on a rough road but steer skillfully to get back on track. If your marriage is dead, you have reached a dead-end. It would be wise to steer to a new relationship or enjoy the new status of being single again.

An effective way not to be stuck in a problem is to redefine it. If you are constantly quarreling with your manager, for instance, the situation may seem hopeless. Why not compromise and explore imaginative ways to collaborate for mutual benefit and work "happily thereafter"?

Why does a student who performs well in math do so poorly in language? The answer may lie in transferring her logical mathematical skills to the study of language. By encouraging her to apply the logical rules of grammar, she would achieve syntax and clarity in communication.

A fivefold approach to problem solving

Problems are best confronted if we approach them not as difficulties but as challenges. Thus, according to James Whitcomb Riley[195] (1849–1916), "The ripest peach is highest on the tree." We must strive to pluck it to taste the fruit.

Many of our affairs hang on a slender thread. Our successes and failures are often the result of accidents. A gold medal might slip away with a small slip on the ice. A tidy sum of money from stocks may be won or lost by only a whisker.

Life is of the same stuff that problems are made of. Hence, there is no escape from them. They are wide-ranging, overwhelming, and sometimes defy solutions. But a silver key can open an iron door, and a heavy load can, with a lever, be lifted lightly.

In 218 BC, Hannibal[196], the famed Carthaginian military general, besieged Rome after a five-month march from Carthage. His soldiers had said there was no way he could cross the Alps with his elephants. He had a brilliant response: "If there is no way," he said, "we will find a way." He did so by discovering an Alpine pass, which enabled him to reach Rome, much to the dismay of the Romans.

Here is a fivefold strategy for problem solving that may help us in difficult circumstances. Vance Packard's "The Hidden Persuaders", cites an interesting story about a mall shoe store owner who turned a loss into a profit through creative problem solving. The whole process occured in five stages.

The first stage was RECOGNITION. The store received a lot of floor traffic from the mall but sales were not keeping pace to the level of other shops. The owner had to realize that there was a problem, because he falsely assumed that many shoppers meant good business.

The second stage was IDENTIFICATION. Among the many problems he faced, the proprietor had to conclude what was the core problem: too much competition from other stores.

The owner then proceeded to stage three, which was to look for SOLUTIONS. He tried many measures. He cut staff and increased advertising of his shoes but none of these efforts seemed to be working. After wrestling with the problem, he reached stage four, when he was convinced that he had discovered the BEST SOLUTION.

On the advice of a marketer, the owner put his emphasis not on selling shoes but in selling an image, particularly for women. His new advertisements barely mentioned shoes but instead promoted a fashionable image, of walking with poise and glamour. These advertisements would appeal to the customers' subliminal thoughts of appearing attractive.

Finally, the shop owner reaches stage five, IMPLEMENTATION. He planned a budget to spend on image advertising and to acquire enough supplies of shoes to cater to increasing demand. He eventually lured in more customers and began to start turning a profit.

A problem is like a garden full of weeds. With patience, we may pluck away the weeds and turn it into a rose garden.

Sometimes, we see the solution only when we clearly understand the problem.
—*Jiddu Krishnamurti (1895–1986)[197]*

A win-win strategy

Winning could be a mark of success, but winning at all costs cannot be a measure of all things. It is true that in our competitive society a high premium is placed on winning, but every winner has a loser and every triumph has a defeat.

Winning has a role to play in sports if, through competition, it leads to excellence. In the area of human interaction, however, fruitful cooperation is preferable to the intense competition that forces people into adversarial positions.

Stephen Covey suggests a win-win strategy in which contending parties identify a common ground or mutuality of interests. He claims that agreements and solutions are deemed fair because they are mutually beneficial and satisfying.

Opposed to this is the win-lose strategy, which is based on power. One party achieves victory at the expense of the other. The losing party may feel bitter and humiliated but lives to fight another day.

A win-win strategy, writes Covey, "is not your way or my way; it is a better way, a higher way."[198]

This strategy is best illustrated in the story of Tim and Emily. They were students who were fiercely competitive, but their grades did not go beyond the mid-seventies. To diffuse tensions they decided to cooperate. Tim concentrated on chapters one, two, and three, and Emily concentrated on chapters four, five, and six, each person acting as a resource to the other. Pleasantly, they were surprised when their grades rose to the high eighties. Both of them turned out to be winners.

Be proactive

> *The future is purchased by the present.*
> —*Dr. Samuel Johnson (1709-1784)*

Changes in society and in our life may occur very unexpectedly. Accidents, sickness, and misfortunes may strike us suddenly and, if unprepared, we may be swept away by them. Prudence demands that we do not remain merely reactive but become proactive. We need to design varying strategies to face different situations as a protection against adverse changes.

In being proactive, the gravity of impending problems is minimized with preventative measures. If they do occur, we are prepared to nip them in the bud. A good example is to be adequately insured against fire, theft, and disaster.

Being proactive shields us against the vicissitudes of life. What is most important is to be enterprising and compromising. Thus, accepting the lesser pain of a wage cut can avert the greater pain of layoff, or the burden of a heavy debt can be lightened through financial restructuring. Even if our relationships are barren, we can reach out to people, and they may respond to us like birds flocking to a fruitful tree.

Climbing the ladder of success

We may state that the ladder of success must rest on the solid grounds of enduring satisfaction and not on the shifting sands of passing pleasures. In climbing the rungs, we must be concerned not only about external riches but also about internal ones, such as enjoying inner peace and calm, as we saw in Chapter 1. The climb should not be wearying but satisfying, ensuring a good quality of life. We should be alert to two possible pitfalls. The first is to aspire much and fail to achieve it. The second, and more serious one, is to aspire to do much and achieve it, only to discover that it was not worth doing.

An altruistic view of success

Many people yearn for a life of comfort or near luxury. Add to it personal advancement, fame, and influence, and our material quest is almost complete. Achieving these goals to some degree is believed to be a mark of material success. People struggle to attain at least a part of them. Some are rewarded; many are not.

Even if we partially fulfill our cherished desires, our satisfaction will be tainted by the ills of society. Imagine living in a resort paradise, but nearby the pollution is so bad that the birds begin to cough.

In the midst of our success, we need to be mindful about the terrible plight of our planet, particularly of the four most serious problems facing the world today. These are the ecological crisis, war and conflict, massive poverty, and the violation of human rights.

An altruistic approach to success would enrich our life and give our idea of success a deeper meaning. We need to be a part of the movement to transform our nation into a green and pleasant land, where the air is fresh, the water is pure, and the soil is unpolluted. Our life is more fulfilling when we see clear blue skies without clouds of smoke and when our parks are adorned with fountains and flowers instead of ugly landscapes.

As our success in life is linked to our prosperity, this happy state cannot, in the long run, be too secure in the midst of massive poverty. Particularly sad is the plight of children. Their short lives are but marches to their graves. Championing a cause, like a second Marshall Plan to aid poor countries, makes our lives more fulfilling.

The widespread violation of human rights is an outrage against human dignity everywhere. Torture, mass rape, executions without trial, child sex slavery, and other inhuman offenses call for immediate action. We must work with humanitarian groups to uphold the rule of law universally, to stop the present crimes against humanity, and to prevent them from occurring again.

An altruistic approach to success may help us lead a more abundant life.

Paradoxes to ponder

Success is never final.[199]
--John Wooden

The obstacle is the path.[200]
--Zen Proverb

Less is more
--Robert Browning

It takes twenty years to make an overnight success.
--Eddie Cantor

We would often be sorry if our wishes were gratified.
--Heraclitus.

178. Bessie Stanley, "What Constitutes Success," *Lincoln Sentinel*, 1905.
179. Morley, Where the Blue Begins.
180. Swift was an Irish satirist, poet, essayist, and cleric. His most famous work was *Gulliver's Travels*, a satire on human nature.
181. King Jr., Martin Luther. "I have a dream," Washington, D.C., August 28, 1963.
182. An English author who was appointed poet laureate.
183. Covey, *The Seven Habits of Highly Effective People*, p. 106.
184. An Italian physicist, astronomer, astrologer, and philosopher, Galileo is closely associated with the scientific revolution.
185. Adapted from Russell Herman Conwell (1843–1925), an American lawyer, author, clergyman, and educator.
186. Though virtually unknown in her lifetime, Dickinson has come to be regarded, along with Walt Whitman, as one of the two quintessential American poets of the nineteenth century.
187. Niebuhr was an American Protestant theologian.
188. A German philosopher, economist, and revolutionary, Marx was the founder of Communism.
189. Adler was an Austrian psychiatrist and psychologist.
190. *The Globe and Mail*, 2005.
191. Hendlin, *When Good Enough Is Never Enough.*
192. Tagore was a poet, playwright, composer, novelist, and Nobel prize winner in literature. His works reshaped Bengali literature and music in the late nineteenth and early twentieth centuries.
193. Pat Conroy, *Beach Music*, Random House 1996.
194. Dr. Sidney B. Simon, professor of psychological education at the University of Massachusetts.
195. Born in Greenfield, Indiana, Riley was an American writer and poet. He was known as the "Hoosier Poet" and the "Children's Poet.".
196. Hannibal, the son of Hamilcar Barca (247 BC– c. 183 BC), was a Punic military commander and politician who later also worked in other professions. He is popularly credited as one of the finest commanders in history..
197. An Indian author and philosopher. For nearly sixty years, Krishnamurti traveled all over the world, pointing out to people the need to transform themselves through self-knowledge, by being aware of their thoughts and feelings in daily life.
198. Covey, *Seven Habits of Highly Effective People,* p. 207.
199. John Wooden, the legendary men's basketball coach at UCLA.
200. Zen proverb.

Chapter 6
Abundant Energy for Daily Life

Chapter 6
Abundant Energy for Daily Life

I. Tapping energy from life around

Cherishing a love for life

My love for nature greatly inspired me to write this book. I have learned to be considerate like the wind. It blows freely on every tree. However busy your life may be, take time to be with nature; it is bound to refresh you.

I enjoyed the splendor of nature in my frequent visits to Algonquin Park, situated about 100 kilometers from Ottawa, Ontario. The infinite variety of nature can best be appreciated by observing the four seasons. Each season impressed me with its own unique beauty, casting a spell on my soul.

A starry sky, sunlight, or moonlight cannot be purchased with money. How exhilarating it is to walk in the woods, feeling the cool breeze blowing down your neck while the sunshine warms your back. How touching it is to be caressed by a loved one, clasped by a baby's hand, or cherished by a friend.

When illness strikes, we are often so resilient. When boredom hits, we seek stimulation by being in the company of good people. Napoleon and the czars would envy us for our standard of living. Their chandeliers had only candles and their carriages were drawn only by horses. They did not have a safety pin, a ballpoint pen, or a radio. Compared with them, how fortunate we are to live today.

In a polluted world, torn by war and woe, most of our problems are man-made, for which there are man-made solutions. We can, if we choose, transform our earth into a green planet, turn our swords into ploughshares, and strive for a just society. In spite of serious setbacks, life has the promise of uplifting us with wonderful energy to be happy and fruitful.

Let nature refresh you

It is calming to the soul to observe how a mountain and a river exist as friendly neighbors. The river seems to glide at its own sweet will, flowing around the mountain, gently caressing its feet.

The mountain stands tall and stately, awesome in its majesty. It exudes a serene silence, yet seems to proclaim that it is acting like a sentinel, protecting the passerby from the dust and ravages of time. The passerby cannot help but feel how immutable is the mountain: solid and rugged, unaffected by clouds of doubt and winds of expediency.

The river, too, can give us a touching experience. As John Gray wrote, life itself resembles a river. While the water remains the same, it is still shifting and changing. Similarly, our life should also constantly be shifting and changing. When the water meets a rock, it does not confront it but gently goes around it. The water shows us that there is a way to get around difficult people.

When our days are weary and tedious, nature adds zest to life. Start by savoring the day's sweetest moment, the dawn. Let the beauty of the rising sun inspire a rising spirit of hope. Let the solemn stillness of the morn inspire a fresh start for a fruitful day. With hope, we become new every day. And when night comes, engage in pleasant conversations, and then go to bed in a pleasant mood.

We are children of nature, and to be one with nature has a therapeutic effect on the soul. As William Hazlitt wrote, "Let us pine for the clear blue sky over our head and a green turf under our feet, a winding road before us and a three hour march to dinner and after that much thinking." [201]

Being one with nature could offer us relief from pollution, traffic jams, and living among concrete forests. A good escape from noise pollution is to soak our ears in three elemental sounds of nature: the sounds of rain, wind and ocean.

It would be wise to remember a cardinal fact: though we live in an artificial world, all things ultimately come from nature, and all things must return to nature. This point is well captured in the words of Omar Khayyám[202]: "I came like water, like wind I go."

Let us at least occasionally return to nature. As Kahil Gibran said, "Let the earth delight to feel your feet, and the wind long to play with your hair."

To savour the seasons is refreshing. How wondrous is the spring. The whole of nature seems to be putting on new, colorful attire. This is the time life reproduces itself. Plants put out new shoots and grow new buds to bear fruit for reproduction. This is the mating season for animals, with birds, in particular, engaging in elaborate courtship. Human beings, too, become more romantic, culminating in festive June weddings. Spring is also the time when farmers sow their fields.

And then we have another miracle when autumn arrives! Fall is as Juvenal[203] says: "The last and sweetest smile of the year, when every leaf looks like a flower." What an abundance of fruits, grains, and varied vegetables there are to relish!

Form a friendship with flowers

We can be one with nature in our friendship with flowers. Flowers soften the harshness of life. In their infinite variety, they convey to us many different subtle messages of wisdom. The sunflower shows us how to be loyal, for example, as it follows the sun even in cloudy weather. The lotus tells us that good comes out of evil; it blooms beautifully as it arises from the mud and dirt. The jasmine tells us a story about vanity; it claims, "Among all flowers no perfume is like mine." The marigold is as colorful as the rose and delicate as the carnation. It is a flower for all seasons. We learn from it to possess the opposite qualities of understanding the summer heat and the evening chill. It is self-reliant and requires little attention. Finally, the chrysanthemum is a flower of many flowers. It tells us that someone who has beauty of soul is likely to have several *other* beautiful qualities.

Thomas Gray[204] (1716–1771) was strolling through the countryside when he was inspired to write, "Many a flower is born to blush unseen, and waste its sweetness in the desert air." The deeper meaning of these lines is that there is many a damsel in a village whose beauty remains unrecognised and hence unrewarded.

An English proverb states that "fair flowers fade fast." This line is more than alliteration, rhythmical though it sounds. The proverb seems to caution that the physical beauty of a person will not last forever. A Japanese proverb goes even further. It states that a "flower that blooms in the morning may wither in the evening."

Fame, power and glory, so highly sought, soon pass away. In fact, all things pass away. That is the essence of wisdom.

Do butterflies come only to pretty flowers? No. They are primarily interested in gathering nectar from any flower. They feed on it and fly away, proudly displaying their beautiful plumage. The lesson we learn from butterflies is that wise people are not primarily attracted by a person's good looks. They are drawn more by a person's sweet disposition.

An appreciation of lilies and lilacs, daisies and pansies brings us closer to nature, and a love for nature brings us closer to wisdom.

Andre Gide[205] (1869–1951) had a suggestion for the seasons. He wrote that he would like to enjoy the summer, flower by flower, as if it were the last one.

Gather nectar from valley and dale

Of all creatures, honeybees are among the most industrious. They fly busily over valley and dale to gather nectar to build their honeycombs.

The relationship between flower and bee seems so naturally beautiful. To the flowers, the bees are welcome visitors, satisfying their yearning to be pollinated. To the bees, the flowers offer nectar and rest. Bees gather nectar from flowers of many kinds. Together, the extracts form a compound for honey that is fresh and delicious.

Nature offers many other examples of cycles and interrelationships among plants, animals, and the elements. In one of the most recognized cycles, sunshine sustains life, water nourishes it, and the wind lends a helping hand in plant reproduction.

This type of interaction is also found among human beings, to an equally amazing degree. While it is true that people do shine when acting individually, they also display excellence when they combine their talents.

What emerges is synergy, whose final outcome is richer than the sum of its parts. This is well demonstrated in the case of a duet. While it is a delight to listen to a tenor and a soprano sing solo, it is equally delightful to hear them perform together. The music of a quartet or a quintet can be more melodious than each of the members performing separately.

With an orchestra, there is a burst of energy as the instruments complement each other in beautiful harmony. The players, while they excel individually, know how to perfectly blend their instruments with others. The violins blend well with the cello, the clarinets with the trumpets, and the tuba with the drums.

The skill and energy of the conductor and the players, working in unison, produce the melodious music. Much energy flows into us when we complement our abilities with those of others.

Networking with people of all kinds is an invaluable resource. Imagine interacting with an assorted group consisting of a dancer, a designer, a doctor, a doorman, and a developer. The insights we gather from this group could fill us with mental energy. We would indeed be like the honeybees, gathering nectar from many flowers. In the process we may also acquire *flashes of wisdom and moments of delight*.

II. Harnessing the energy within us

Transform emptiness into fulfillment

When we enjoy life to the fullest, it is often possible to be brimming with energy. One way to attain this is to get into a "comfort zone," as described by John Roger and Peter McWilliams.[206]

We need our comfort zone to counteract feelings of emptiness that may strike us from time to time. No person is immune to them because they are part of the human condition. We experience this when we really do not know what we want and when we have no clear idea how we feel. These are generally passing sensations, which we can overcome by accentuating our comfort zone and feeling fully alive.

Roger and McWilliams explain the comfort zone as our personal area of thoughts and actions within which we are at ease. The zone includes all actions we have accomplished of which we are proud and all thoughts we count as precious. The authors argue that the comfort zone is the core of our being, our soul, and foundation for behavior. This conviction is certainly worthy of our consideration.

If we take a critical view of the comfort zone, it is evident that this concept is not always obvious. Our perceptions of people and events could be mistaken, plunging us into a "twilight zone." Many times we have rested comfortably with the conviction that people are true and upright, only to discover, to our amazement, that they are the opposite. The comfort zone is therefore a useful concept only if we consider it in relative terms.

Unleashing the brain's enormous power

"No other word better describes the human brain than the term *"amazing"*.

We generally think we have one brain, but really it is divided into two hemispheres acting somewhat independently, performing distinctly different functions. They combine to act as one system while preserving differentiated responses. For example, experiments show that injury to the left side of the brain results in very different effects than injury to the right side.

The left side is prone to have scientific qualities, such as a tendency to be objective and precise. Thus "left-brain" people process information sequentially and logically. They prefer to deal with concrete data rather than nebulous or unstructured information. They like to work in a step-by-step fashion and complete a project before going on to another. They dislike clutter and like their work to be well planned and organized. Professions that attract left-brain people are accounting, computing, engineering, and the physical sciences.

The right side tends to have artistic qualities, like a talent for music and painting. This leads to "right-brain" people being energized by different sets of conditions. They enjoy change and flexible schedules as well as working spontaneously and intuitively. They tend to be inventive and imaginative. They are adept at problem solving and are good at conceptualisation. They are generalists and prefer to look at the entire picture rather than at the details.

Professions that lure right-brain people are the arts, counseling, religion, and writing.

We must avoid the pitfall of an either/or perspective that claims one side of the brain is superior to the other. The qualities of the two hemispheres need not be opposed. On the contrary, they complement each other harmoniously. Dr. Anne McGee[207] writes, "Striking a balance between the two hemispheres is the most productive and creative way to live."

The combined resources of both sides enrich a person immensely. Perhaps the most important effect is the unleashing of abundant energy for everyday living: energy to look at life afresh; energy to be hopeful and confident; and energy to climb effortlessly the steep hills of existence. Thus, we become a well-rounded personality, leading a joyful life with sparks of wisdom.

Finessing Type A and B personalities

In 1974 two Harvard cardiologists, Dr. Meyer Friedman and Dr. Ray H. Rosenman, published a best seller entitled *Type A Behavior and Your Heart*. Since then, numerous studies have confirmed that, while a Type A personality possesses several desirable qualities, pursuing them in excess raises the risk of cardiac ailments. The authors also claim that a Type B personality is less prone to heart disease.

There is no absolute difference between Type A and B personalities. They share common patterns and differ only in degree. As we explained in Chapter 2 about the Differential Principle, the distinction between Type A and B personalities is not one of kind but one of degree.

Type A personalities are well admired for being highly successful. Efficient and productive, they display skill in planning, organizing, and in time management. Disciplined and hard-working, they are bold and enterprising. To Type A personalities, achieving success is highly prized.

Who, then, is a wholesome Type A personality, one who leads a successful life without paying a high price? We find the answer in a person who embodies, to some degree, the principle of balance and proportion that we discussed in detail in Chapter 2.

This principle is observed in a dance, and life itself is like a dance. Skillfully, we may choreograph it to reflect both strength and suppleness. We must sometimes walk on tiptoe or leap over hurdles with great energy. A slip or a mistake could ruin the dance.

We need to finesse Type A and B personalities with the exquisite skills of a dancer. We could be ambitious but not blindly so; competitive but not fierce; assertive but not abrasive; and aggressive if necessary but never ruthless.

We must also restrain ourselves from being cynical, mistrustful, or suspicious. At the same time, we should display more understanding and altruism. Occasionally, we may get a little angry or irritated, but we should generally remain calm and collected.

When choreographing our personality, our judgment should be selective. As the situation demands, we may have to display opposite qualities. Thus, it is appropriate to be dominant when exercising conciliatory leadership in order to be persuasive.

If a Type A personality does not finesse his behavior and the negative aspects are very pronounced, the effects can be serious. An extreme consequence is hostility that is toxic. The nervous system becomes out of balance. It starts to secrete an excess amount of stress hormones and chemicals and then inhibits the secretion of other hormones and chemicals that would normally help a person cool down. The final result is engine failure or what doctors call a heart attack.

A Type B personality has the opposite qualities of a Type A. Like the tortoise winning the race, the Type B may ultimately prevail. He may live to enjoy the fruits of his labor, unlike certain Type A personalities, who rush from success to success only to drop dead at an early age. A Type B personality possesses many desirable qualities. He is placid, at peace with himself, savors time, and does not miss out on the finer things of life.

In a good part of our life, we need to be in a Rest Mode. Among other features, our heart beats gently and our blood pressure is normal. However, the demands of living may require us to be ever alert and vigilant. To meet these challenges, our system gets into a Go Mode.

The Go Mode (Fight-or-Flight Response)	The Rest Mode (Relaxation Response)
You sense danger	You feel at ease
Adrenalin surges	Adrenalin decreases
Heart rate quickens	Heart rate slows down
Blood pressure rises	Blood pressure falls
Breathing is high, shallow	Breathing deepens
Blood thickens	Blood normalizes
Blood flow is diverted	Blood flows to extremities
Muscles tense	Muscles relax
Sweat is produced	Sweating decreases
Digestion slows down	Digestion normalizes

Sex hormones decrease	Sex hormones increase
Immunity is suppressed	Immunity is strengthened

Each mode has its intended functions. Neither is bad nor good in all situations. The question is, which mode are you in most of the time? And can you shift into the Rest Mode when your system needs rest?

A positive outlook adds vigor to life

According to Elwood N. Chapman,[208] "An attitude is the way we look at the world around us. It is how we view our environment and our future." Our attitudes are exclusively ours. They shape our conduct, our work, our relationships, and every aspect of life. They provide a powerful tool to gain control over our life. We need not, as Henry David Thoreau wrote, "lead lives of quiet desperation" due to lack of control.

Our attitudes make each of us unique. Proper attitudes are priceless, too, because they determine our happiness in life.

Chapman presents impressive evidence that negative attitudes dissipate energy. It would be a mark of wisdom to acquire a permanent, positive outlook. Endowed with this outlook, we would likely be vibrant in our endeavors, and our prospects would appear pleasing.

The power to lift one's spirit is needed to offset the spirit that pulls us down. Negative attitudes could strike anyone at anytime. They are like a gloomy cloud that blocks our vision and prevents us from seeing the sunny side of life. Skepticism, cynicism, fear, and hopelessness are negative emotions that stall us into inaction.

Here is a plan on how to counteract negative forces with positive forces.

Cultivate a positive self-image
- Forming a favorable self-image helps you form other favorable self-concepts.
- Healthy self-esteem helps you to like yourself and thereby like others.
- Self-respect gives you dignity and encourages others to respect you.

Try to imitate the sundial. It counts only the sunny hours.

Positive relationships help foster a positive self-image. Such relationships may include friends, relatives, acquaintances, and associates. Our interaction with them could be emotional, productive, and satisfying to various degrees.

Our emotional interaction could make us feel exuberant. Our productive interaction could make us feel energetic. To be in such a state could help us enjoy a glimpse of wisdom.

Positive relationships are a treasure. They need to be constantly renewed, strengthened, and savored. They cannot, however, be taken for granted.

A common shortcoming is neglect, which may lead to tensions and misunderstandings. When they occur, it is best to be proactive. Ever watchful for the yellow traffic signal, we need to act forcefully, to restore the happy state of a relationship.

It is a fact of life that there are difficult people in this world. Such people are a drain on our energy. It is wise to avoid them or even flee from them. If this is not possible, we have to learn to endure them. Fortunately, our powerful positive attitudes act like an immune system, warding off the negativism of negative people.

It makes good sense to love those who love you.

Enthusiasm: the wine of life

Boredom in our society is a serious problem. It can affect everyone: the young, the old, the rich, the poor, and even the highly successful. A cure for boredom is curiosity. To further combat boredom, we need enthusiasm to lift us out of monotony and dull routine. When the novelty of things wears off, even a hero becomes a bore. Many people were not that thrilled by a second lunar landing, for instance.

While boredom is inevitable, the sources of enthusiasm are inexhaustible. We marvel at the beauties of the deep sea as they are revealed to us through film, and we wonder at the North Star twinkling in the sky.

Life is sometimes boring, yet it is possible to be enthusiastic in many areas. Domestic chores become less onerous if accompanied by toe-tapping music. At our places of employment, the burden of work is no burden if we anticipate rewarding prospects. In his book *Enthusiasm Makes a Difference*, Norman Vincent Peale claims that enthusiasm is often a factor that distinguishes excellence from mediocrity and success from failure. We may argue that enthusiasm mitigates fear, worry, and a host of other negative emotions. It will be beneficial to also look for little joys that refresh us constantly.

Thus, we may state that enthusiasm is the wine of life. If anything, it is a wine of rare vintage that should still be sipped often to energize our behavior and brighten our days.

One way to achieve enthusiasm and energy is to be well balanced and have a well-integrated personality. In this state our thoughts, feelings, and actions are entirely one and together move in one direction. In real-life situations, it is not uncommon for people to achieve this integration. Consider the example of how palliative care nurses bring their minds to bear on their patients, all the while displaying great empathy and performing their duties efficiently.

Time out to replenish and renew

A frenzied life may shorten life. Hectic activity not balanced by rest and leisure may not be very productive. Evidence reveals that workaholism could affect our health very adversely. According to Dr. Phillip Johnson,[209] frantic activity of the human system is like an engine racing at a hectic pace. The high speed cannot be sustained for long without danger to the system. The engine must come to a halt to be refueled and retuned before it hits the road again.

The idea of time out, so familiar in sports, is a useful concept to apply to human behavior. Just as athletes take time out to regroup during a game, in the larger game of life we need to take time out for fun and leisure.

Life is a challenge. Its unceasing demands may take a toll on us, resulting in burnout. For this reason we need to set apart special time for ourselves to engage in a variety of enjoyable activities. We need to replenish our energy and renew our spirit.

In a remarkable passage, Henry David Thoreau wrote, "It is the marriage of the soul with nature that makes the intellect fruitful, and gives birth to imagination."[210]

In savoring some of the infinite variety of nature, we banish boredom and energize our behavior. What is refreshing is the variety of changes that rotate in an orderly way. The alternation of a hot day followed by a cool night, or the alternation of summer and winter gradually ushered in by the spring and autumn, is pleasing to the mind and body.

As Louis Armstrong (1901–1971) sang, "I see trees of green, red roses too, I see them bloom, for me and you, and I think to myself, what a wonderful world."[211]

Finally, there are skylarks and canaries singing at dawn to provide us a heavenly concert.

Leisure gives us rest from stress and energizes our spirit. Relaxing in a garden, which is a delight for the eye, provokes many good ideas day after day.

It would be so energizing to walk in the highlands watching deer or in the lowlands smelling flowers. It is energizing to renew old acquaintances, paint silver linings on pictures of clouds, and clown with little children, driving them to peals of laughter.

In the midst of a busy life, it is wise to take time out to think and to reflect about our future and ourselves. In a word, we must *renew* ourselves.

Nothing remains the same because everything is changing. Wisdom demands that we adjust to changes by discarding clichés and accepting new perspectives to suit new realities. In a sense, we have to be reborn or renew ourselves emotionally and intellectually.

In this renewal, we may discover that enthusiasm is the wine of life, a source of immense energy. Anything has the potential to generate enthusiasm, whether it's making a coat of many colors, viewing a fine film, or, as Gene Kelly did, singing in the rain.

Our mind is like a clock that is always running down. It must be rewound.

Be swift and slow

People often rush to do things in a needless waste of energy. For instance, it is common in air travel for passengers to disembark impatiently, but then wait at the baggage counter very patiently.

Accomplishing a task speedily is not always the best way of doing it. Canadian writer Carl Honoré, in his book, *In Praise of Slow*,[212] borrows a point from Goethe that a runaway horse has speed from a human perspective, but it counts for nothing. On the other hand, a well-trained equestrian horse is able to trot elegantly and race speedily to the finish line. Always doing things speedily is not the best way of doing them and can be counterproductive. Class and quality are achieved through greater planning and proceeding at a lesser pace.

Living is like running a marathon: when we rush through life, we are like the runner sprinting the marathon. For a while he is ahead, but soon the speed takes a toll on him and he collapses from exhaustion.

There are many cases of professional men and women who attained great success and wealth but did not live long to enjoy the fruits of their hard work.

Striking a balance between a swift and slow pace will help us to conserve energy. In some situations we need to proceed at a measured pace, as in the work of an architect, a master craftsman, or a choreographer. In other situations, we need to act swiftly because timing is of the essence. A good example of this is the work of a stock trader. Decisions have to be made within seconds because they can make a difference between a gain or a loss of millions of dollars.

Life is so complex that we must be flexible to respond to challenges in an appropriate way. A judicious combination of a slow and swift pace whenever the occasion demands is perhaps the best approach to be productive. While a hectic life may be beneficial in the short run, it cannot be sustained in the long run without the risk of harming ourselves. Workaholics do achieve great results, but they eventually pay a high price.

A sad consequence of living out of balance is burnout. In a typical case, a person will say, "I wake up tired and go to bed tired." He thinks it's productive when his days are all work and no play, but the day of reckoning does come.

Gradually, a range of symptoms creeps in. He is ill motivated, his enthusiasm wanes, and he suffers from a lack of interest and a lack of energy. He may even show little appetite for sex or emotional expressions.

Fortunately, a range of remedies is available to come out of this rut. We must zero in on the few positive things going for us and gradually build up our energy and enthusiasm. Good friends and good music, lots of laughter and lots of leisure, may help us on the road to recovery.

It is wise to go slow to conserve our energy.

III. Energy from human interaction

Manage your time energetically

Time management is crucially important. We must avoid the pitfall of losing life, minute by minute, day by day, in a hundred different ways.

Although time is the stuff of life, it is wise to govern the clock and not be governed by it. Jim Loehr and Tony Schwartz claim that energy, and not time, is our most precious resource. In *The Power of Full Engagement*, they introduce this bold concept, claiming that "performance, health and happiness are grounded in the skilful management of energy."[213]

While efficient time management is important because time is limited, the quantity and quality of *energy* is not so limited. In fact, energy could be of greater importance, according to the authors, because it can be renewed and expanded in four realms—physical, emotional, mental, and spiritual. These sources of energy, flowing from each of the realms, interact and reinforce each other. The total energy generated has a tremendous impact on our lives.

Physically, we expand our energy through strength, stamina, and suppleness, as we saw in Chapter 4. Emotionally, there is a mysterious energy of love in forming intimate relationships among members of the family, as we saw in Chapter 3. Mentally, we generate great energy by harnessing the power of the brain; and spiritually, we enjoy a quiet energy that emanates from a philosophical view of life.

Certain types of behavior do manifest themselves in all of the four realms. A genial spirit, a generous gesture, and a hopeful attitude can affect our body and soul simultaneously. These behaviors release chemicals in the brain that calm the limbic system, which has a healthy effect on the body. There is a scientific basis for the value of energizing ourselves by being loving and giving, good and kind. The opposite of this is also true. Those who are sometimes unkind are deprived of these positive chemicals and may lack energy.

An effective way to lessen the loss of energy is to minimize negative attitudes. Although it is human to possess them to some degree, an overwhelming negative outlook is injurious. Anger, fear, and pessimism are common shortcomings that deprive us from displaying the best of ourselves.

We can keep them well under control by practicing calmness, courage, and optimism.

A pleasant mood opens doors

A mood is an emotional state that lasts a long time. Robert E. Thayer describes a mood "as a background feeling that persists over time."[214] He further suggests that understanding and controlling everyday moods can add substantially to the pleasures of living. Our moods lie at the very core of our life. They can determine how active and enterprising we can become, or how slow and lethargic we may be.

Fortunately, there are only a few basic moods: joyful, angry, and anxious. Others are variations. When we are in a pleasant mood, doing a difficult task becomes easy. When we are in an unpleasant mood, even an easy task appears difficult. The Book of Proverbs expresses the same idea eloquently: "When man is gloomy, everything seems to go wrong; when he is cheerful, everything seems right!"[215] For our mental well-being, it is important to shy away from negative moods and transform them into finer moods.

A good mood fills us with energy and enthusiasm. It frees us from anxiety and depression and transforms our negative attitudes into a positive outlook. Life itself becomes happy and satisfying. A certain sign of wisdom is cheerfulness.

Of course, it is impossible to be in a good mood all the time. The vicissitudes of life may at times compel us to be melancholy, but we come out of it through the power of laughter. Man is reputedly the only creature endowed with the capacity to laugh. Charles Lamb[216] (1775–1834) wrote that a laugh is worth more than a hundred groans. An ability to smile often is like sunshine to flowers.

Wit and comedy have a relaxing effect, and even a straw that tickles could become an instrument of happiness. Of particular importance is the ability to engage in self-deprecation. As G. K. Chesterton said, men should imitate the angels, who are able to fly because they do not take themselves too seriously.

One must strive to maintain a pleasant mood, which will open doors and have an energizing effect. A good example of a positive attitude is how mourners cope with bereavement in New Orleans. When a jazz musician dies, his funeral is celebrated with dancing and the best of jazz music. It is a final farewell to a brother musician. It is also aimed to divert grief and help the mourners cope with the loss. Through right thinking, the folks in New Orleans are able to bow gracefully to the departure of a loved one.

Sometimes our reactions to life events are more important than the events themselves. Wisdom suggests that we should strive to achieve a persistent pleasant mood. Such a mood endows us with a gentle temperament, which becomes an integral part of our personality.

Make relationships more endearing

When we have a conviction that people care about us, we get a soothing sensation in our soul. We seem to glow with warmth and security. We savor the fact that we are recognized and wanted. In that positive emotional state, we cannot feel left out.

The response of others, however, depends on our own initiative and efforts. We cannot expect others to be nice and warm to us unless we have made the first moves. To get a friend, we must become a friend. To obtain understanding, we must show understanding. To receive affection, we must give affection.

Old friends are critical. They are like old wine, old gold, and old books; they get better with time. It would be wise to renew the best of old acquaintances and strengthen the best of new acquaintances. One matter on which all of humanity agrees is the value of friendship, because it is mutually beneficial. It is this value that prompted Samuel Taylor Coleridge to write that friendship is like a sheltering tree.

Jane Austen wrote that friendship is the finest balm for the pangs of disappointment. When our personal relationships are rich and endearing, we have something worthy and noble that brings joy to ourselves and others.

When people concentrate all their efforts to promote their own interests, they soon get bored. On the contrary, when their interests are broad and genuinely involved in the aims and aspirations of others, life can become exciting.

Alfred Adler claimed that the true meaning of life lies in contributing to the good of others. If we look around us, we see the contribution that our ancestors have made in the fields of art, science, human welfare, and innumerable other areas. We have immensely benefited from their contributions, and now it is our turn to contribute to our own generation.

Contributions to life also contribute to human happiness. A happy person is at harmony with himself. He has an ability to fight and overcome whatever disturbs his peace of mind. He also possesses a great capacity to overcome boredom.

Inevitably, one will encounter difficult people. Try facing them by emulating the Japanese proverb: "Be like the cherry tree. It covers with flowers the hand that shakes it."

Learn a new art or craft

Mastering the art of pottery offers much satisfaction. It is one of the oldest arts, dating back to Babylonian times, about five thousand years ago. Through works of pottery, we may express ourselves by leaving a mark of our personality and our unique way of seeing things. For instance, we may design a deer with a nose glowing in red or portray a ballerina in a graceful pose. As amateur artists, we could adorn our pottery by combining the spectrum of colors in light. We could even go further by having the fun of experimenting with various shades of the seven colors.

Pottery is popular today because we can begin by designing a simple structure and later advance to create a more sophisticated sculpture. Pottery, like other arts, offers an opportunity for self-expression—a vital human need that leads to self-fulfillment.

After intense mental activity, it would be relaxing to walk in the woods in search of a natural wooden sculpture, using a knife or axe with the touch of an artist. It is challenging to transform a branch, a stem, or a trunk to look like a bird, a deer, or a dancer.

Trying something new requires a spirit of adventure. Johnny was the only man to enroll in a class for belly dancing consisting of thirty women. His presence amused some and intrigued others. While the dancers wriggled their bellies in a natural poise, Johnny cut an awkward figure. He, however, considered his adventure as a positive learning experience that enriched his life. He was proud that he dared to enter "a charming den," and he enjoyed the laughter he provoked among his friends.

We can experience a sense of adventure by observing how nature abounds with examples of cooperation among plants, animals, and the elements. The wind directs the clasping ivy where to climb. and does it blows less harshly on the sheared sheep? In a forest, thick vegetation interweaves at the top to form a protective canopy. Thanks to the canopy, rains do not fall too heavily, and animals escape the intensity of the sun because its fierce rays are well filtered.

The interrelationship among life forms and their connection to the elements benefits all life. Biologists refer to this phenomenon as symbiosis. Social scientists have applied this concept to human behavior. While individual initiative and enterprise are valued, the combination of two or more talented people produces powerful synergy. In a complex surgical operation, for instance, a team of surgeons, physicians, and nurses combine their expertise in a race against the clock. Their synergy saves patients from the jaws of death.

Savour new interests

Cultivating a outside new interest outside your field, can add spark to you life. You have a wide range to choose, from astronomy to aviation, archery, cycling, dancing, philately and sailing.

I have chosen anthropology because it stirs new interests about people, such as the Pygmies, the Laps, the Bedouins, and the Gypsies. When we compare and contrast modern society with traditional societies, we can better appreciate the merits and shortcomings of both groupings.

An anthropological study of traditional, non-agricultural people is fascinating. In understanding their way of living, we gather a deep insight about human nature and the evolution of our behavior. What is more striking about our ancient ancestors was their spirit of exploration. They were restless; they did not stay long in one place, but boldly trekked to new areas in search of food and more hospitable environments.

In a remarkable passage, Alfred Whitehead[217] (1861–1947) attributed the ascendancy of man to his *wandering nature*. An intense urge to explore compelled him to traverse vast distances only by foot and by water. About ten thousand years ago, our ancestors started a long process of accomplishing an astonishing odyssey. They eventually explored and inhabited of the entire expanse of North and South America. The process no doubt took a few millennia, but the marks they left behind are still seen to this day. Ruins and artefacts have been found even in the most remote parts of the Americas.

The wandering nature of ancient man is, to some degree, still observed today among the Inuit people. Though their nomadic features are not significant today, in the past their wandering characteristics were amazing. They founded settlements by trekking to vast distances in two continents. They inhabited the Arctic regions of Alaska, Canada, Greenland, Sweden, Finland, and Siberia. In all these diverse territories today, they are of similar ethnic stock, speaking—with some variations—the same Inuit language. They are indeed a true circumpolar people. Living as they did in a cold and harsh environment, they cultivated impressive survival skills through a process of sharing and cooperation. The extended family was the principal social unit, and through teamwork the Inuit engaged in hunting, fishing, trapping, and building houses. This process equipped them to dominate the Arctic animal world and confront the elements.

The Pygmies are another type of traditional, non-agricultural people who live in the rain forests of Central Africa, particularly in Rwanda, Burundi, and the Democratic Republic of Congo. Their remarkable survival is attributed to the process of sharing and cooperation. The Pygmies are mainly hunters and food gatherers and have resisted attempts by governments to force them into farming.

They average less than five feet in stature and are extremely industrious. They lead a communal life and are very proud of their culture.

We saw in Chapter 2 that it is almost a universal law for people to strictly adhere to the customs of their culture, whether they are the Bushmen in the Kalahari Desert, the Sammis in Scandinavia, or the Amish in Pennsylvania. People are governed by their culture from birth to death. It is like an invisible garment they wear all their lives.

As culture is so intimately intertwined with the lives of people, they become very jealous and protective of their culture. They consider it unique, and when they are intolerant of other cultures, tensions arise, which can lead to bitter conflict.

The shaman is a fascinating figure. Through an understanding of his historical role in ancient societies, we understand the roots of modern society. The shaman is the father of many of our modern institutions. The educator, the physician, the priest, the ruler, and the social worker owe their origin to the shaman. The shaman is still very much alive today, holding a dominant position among several tribes in Africa and South America.

The evolution of society from ancient times coincided with the separation and specialization of the many functions of the shaman. We can better appreciate modern institutions like the church and state, where we traced how they have progressed from primitive origins.

High energy from high ideals

Positive thoughts like joy, happiness and worthiness, produce positive results like enthusiasm, calm and well being. Negative thoughts like mistrust, unworthiness and fear, produce negative results like tension, anxiety and fatigue.

High ideals are like stars in the dark sky. We may never reach them, but like the North Star, they provide a sense of direction. We saw in Chapter 1 that the noble ideal of magnanimity was first expounded by Aristotle and reiterated over the centuries. A magnanimous spirit denotes a generous attitude and a capacity to forgive and forget those who have wronged us; earning their good will is our main concern.

Aristotle attributed a more important meaning to magnanimity, which pertains to bestowing material benefits on others. He asserted that a finer quality of life would be reached if we enhance our resources or increase our wealth to be in a better position to help others. In modern terms, magnanimity entails using our excess wealth as a trust, primarily for the sake of benefiting others. Modern philanthropy, to some degree, embodies this principle. At the individual level, a spirit of magnanimity energizes our life.

When the apathy of people disheartens us, we are heartened by the warmth of those who are friendly to us.

While boredom saps our energy, enthusiasm invigorates our life. Ralph Waldo Emerson claimed that nothing great was ever achieved without enthusiasm. John Wanamaker[218] (1838–1922) said, "Every man is at his best when he adds enthusiasm to whatever he honestly believes in."

It is wise to be both subjective and objective. While certain areas, like morality or sexuality, lend themselves to debate, there are other areas in which a scientific approach is refreshing. In geometry or calculus, for instance, there are no national or sectarian versions. A universal consensus prevails regarding their validity. In the midst of controversies, the acceptance of universal values is energizing. We need to more fully accept universal values, which are a force for unity and good. The principle of the rule of law and the *Universal Declaration of Human Rights* are high ideals worthy of advancement.

Another lofty idea that enlivens our spirit is to become an inspiration for goodness among others. According to this Socratic ideal, our many acts of kindness and generosity are designed to provoke others to act in the same loving manner. Realistically, only a few might respond in equal measure, while others may remain lukewarm or not react at all. This is human nature.

The words of Jesus Christ have been inspiring to millions. To those who are crushed by burdens, he promises, "Come unto me, all ye that labour and are heavy laden, and I will give you rest."[219] To those who are forgiving, he says, "Blessed are the merciful: for they shall obtain mercy."[220] And to people who grieve, he says, "Blessed are they that mourn: for they shall be comforted."[221]

To people depressed by man's inhumanity to man, the message of the Buddha is consoling: universal compassion gives hope, easing the pain of human suffering and transforming the stranger into a brother.

To people troubled by war and conflict arising over ethnic and cultural differences, the message of the Koran is uplifting. It proclaims that, ultimately, "All people belong to one nation."

In modern times, H. G. Wells, the visionary, expressed the sublime idea that "Our true nationality is mankind."

What is common to all these noble ideas is that all the peoples of the world are fellow human beings. Only accidentally are they African, Asian, European, or from the Americas.

Paradoxes to ponder

> For fast-acting relief, try slowing down.
> --Lily Tomlin

> Hasten slowly (in Latin, 'Festina lente')
> -- Augustus Caesar, Quoted by Suetonius (first century A.D.)

201 Hazlitt was an English literary critic (1778-1830).

202. Omar Khayyám (1048–1131) was a Persian poet, mathematician, and astronomer.

203. Juvenal was a Roman poet of the first century.

204. Thomas Gray was an English poet and classical scholar.

205. Gide, a French writer, won the Nobel Prize for literature.

206. Roger and MacWilliams, *Comfort Zone*.

207. Dr. Ann McGee-Cooper is a business consultant and author.

208. Chapman, *Attitude: Your Most Priceless Possession*.

209. Johnson, *Time Out*.

210. Thoreau, *Journal*, Aug. 21, 1851.

211. Bob Thiele and George David Weiss. "What a Wonderful World," 1967, Armstrong was perhaps the greatest of all jazz musicians. He defined what it was to play jazz.

212. Honoré, *In Praise of Slow*, 2004.

213. Loehr and Schwartz, *The Power of Full Engagement*, p.3.

214. Thayer, *The Origin of Everyday Moods*.

215. Proverbs 15:15, TLB.

216. Lamb was an English essayist best known for his *Essays of Elia* and for the children's book *Tales from Shakespeare*.

217. Whitehead was a British mathematician, logician, and philosopher.

218. Wanamaker, an American merchant, is viewed as the father of modern advertising.

219. Matthew 11:28, KJV.

220. Matthew 5:7, KJV.

221. Matthew 5:4, KJV.

Conclusion

I wish to present to you a "gift" that I hope you will treasure all your life. I want you to cultivate an "inner eye," which will help you gather rich insights about human behavior and human society. It has helped me immensely, and I want it to help you as well.

In Chapter 1 we saw with our inner eye that differences in reality are not of kind, but of degree. Look at the beautiful rainbow. Its seven colors cannot be clearly separated because they blend into each other, such as a tinge of bluish red and a reddish blue. This inner eye will help you to fine-tune your judgment and draw clear distinctions in the behavior of people. With it, you will find that there are kind and unkind people to various degrees, so much so that no two individuals are alike.

We saw in Chapter 2 that with your inner eye, you will gather a deep perspective which, after you are born, you begin to wear as an invisible garment. It entirely shapes your thinking and hence your behavior, for better or for worse. You and I are products of our culture. It requires the inner eye to understand that some of our cultural practices might be wrong and some practices of others might be right.

In Chapter 3 we saw with our inner eye that, while all things pass away, love alone endures. We also saw that an important aspect of romantic love is reproduction, which is indeed a marvelous process. The entire living world, ranging from the tiny amoeba to the mighty blue whale, is governed by the universal law to propitiate itself.

While I can see the splendor of nature with my naked eye, I also see nature's wondrous design for reproduction with my inner eye. The process by which plant reproduction takes place, with the cooperation of wind, water, and animals, is amazing.

Among animals, the design for reproduction is even more marvelous. Courtship among birds is long. It includes dances and love songs containing notes of diverse sharps and octaves. Among mammals, note the splendid designs for reproduction. In the deer family, for instance, males grow elegant antlers as a form of sexual allure. The universal desire for all forms of life to propagate themselves is one of the wonders of nature. It reaches its perfection among human beings. The design is reinforced through sexual allusions in many areas of life, including advertising, music, painting, sculpture, and literature.

In Chapter 4 my inner eye shifted to look at the world through the eyes of a child. What I discovered is that a child's wisdom is also wisdom. Some

187

elevated thoughts that come spontaneously to a child are not so evident to adults. At a multicultural school in Toronto, I observed how children of diverse color and ethnic background interacted in peace and friendship. On the contrary, it requires the inner eye among adults to appreciate the cardinal fact that all the peoples of the world belong to the same human family. If people could grasp this fact, there would be peace in the world.

Networking with people provides an invaluable resource for sharpening your inner eye, as we saw in Chapter 5. In my college days, four students and I decided to divide the history course into five time periods. While all of us had a general idea of the course, each of us specialized in one time period. Mine was World War II, and I gathered the insight through my inner eye how the First World War led to the second. I also found that the Second World War was an unnecessary war, given that history had already tragically demonstrated how one war usually leads to another. Similarly, my colleagues made noteworthy contributions.

While I see with my naked eye the external beauty of people, I admire with my inner eye their internal beauty. It is a beauty of the soul; an attribute possessed by people of all ages and backgrounds. On reflecting, I discovered, as in Chapter 6, that human action is beautiful when it is accomplished with energy. Whether they are painting, conversing, dancing, or singing, the faces of people seem to glow when they are engaged in satisfying endeavors.

We need the inner eye to observe the subtle energy displayed by people when they are in a pleasant mood doing pleasant things. I know a woman who spent long hours with children but never seemed to tire because she was always exuberant. I found among others, and also within myself, that positive outlook and a high self-esteem add vigor to life. Self-esteem is associated with self-confidence and self-reliance. These are qualities that can energize you and me.

I think an ideal life or a perfect person can never be found, but I present them to you in this book in small fragments. A semblance of perfection can adorn our life if we imitate the perfection in nature. We can learn from the river and the mountain, how they exist side by side as friendly neighbours and how the river never flows backwards but progresses toward the sea.

Sometimes nature is imperfect and violent, causing a lot of human misery. While learning to cope with these changes, we may still remain calm and admire the perfection that prevails in nature.

Consider the wonder of a tree. The leaves are closely knit, yet in a marvelous way they share the open space to welcome the sun. Each leaf seems "mindful" of its sister leaf in not blocking the friendly sun (see the diagram of the leaf below).

Similarly, it is natural for people to share, to be mindful of others and not block their desire to live. Albert Schweitzer ministered to lepers in Africa and shared with them everything he had. Anne Frank, the twelve-year-old Dutch girl who kept a diary during the Nazi occupation of her country, displayed exemplary heroism. She readily forgave the Nazis before her execution. Her goodness shines to this day. Among ordinary people, there are millions whose sacrificial love is extraordinary.

I do not think we shall ever have a perfect world, but an improving world is possible or even probable. Just as a garden full of fruits, flowers, and fragrances contains some weeds, among difficult people we find many others who are beautiful. Christ said that we will find the wheat with the chaff.[231]

Leading a perfect life is like having heaven on earth, which is never possible. We can, however, fill our life with moments of heaven. Savoring the loving embrace of a loved one or listening to music that stirs your soul, for instance, can give you deep delight.

Life is fragile. It hangs like a dewdrop on the tip of a leaf. To surmount the brevity of our days, we need to consume the fullness of life in the charms of nature, in art, and in human goodness.

My little discourse is now concluded. What I said in the beginning I wish to state at the end: plant a tree of Wisdom and Delight and enjoy its growth all your life.

One last word. The following quote from Michel de Montaigne best reflects my own thinking: "I have gathered a posey of other men's flowers, but nothing but the thread that binds them, is my own."

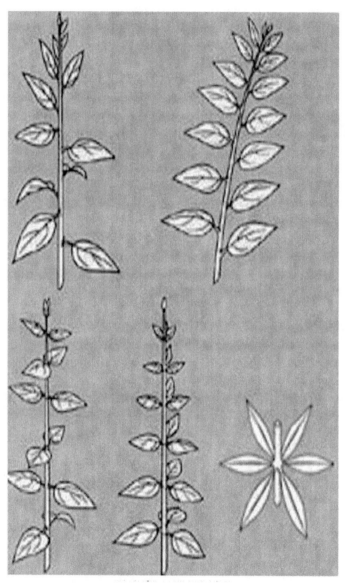

One leaf covers not another.

Appendix A
Criteria to gauge biological age

Aerobic Capacity
Antioxidant Levels
Auditory Threshold
Blood Pressure
Blood Sugar Regulation
Body Fat
Bone Density
Cholesterol and Lipid Levels
Hormonal Levels
Immune Function
Metabolic Activity
Muscle Mass
Muscle Strength
Skin Thickness
Temperature Regulation
Visual Threshold

Index

Vitamin 118–120
Vulnerable 7, 21

W

Walking 8, 24, 39, 60, 129–131, 158
Wanamaker, John 184
Wants 15, 32, 154
Water 15, 17, 21, 25, 30, 33, 53,
         67–68, 90, 113, 130, 148–149,
         153, 161, 168, 170, 182, 187
Watt, James 45
Wei ji 156
Well
  balanced 6, 81, 176
  integrated 6, 55
Wells, H. G. 185
West, Mae 56
Whitehead, Alfred 182
Whitman, Walt 70, 163, 209
Wilde, Oscar 56, 100
Williams, Williams Carlos 18
Wit 18, 33, 56, 58, 63, 66, 75, 155
Withstand 19, 90
Wonder 2, 16, 26, 50, 68, 98, 107–
         108, 151, 175, 188
Wooden, John 162–163
Wordsworth, William 24, 33, 103,
         109, 206, 209
World 5, 6, 10, 12–21, 24–27, 29–31,
         35, 39–40, 44, 48–50, 54–55,
         60–64, 68, 70, 75–76, 78, 81,
         84–87, 89, 97–98, 107–108,
         110, 118, 130, 132, 143, 147,
         150, 152–153, 161, 163,
         167–168, 174–176, 183, 185,
         187–189

Y

Yoga 122, 128, 139, 211

Z

Zebra 26
Zinc 113, 119, 120–122

Current Bibliography

Allan, Robert, with Blass, Donna. *Getting Control of Your Anger.* New York: McGraw Hill, 2006

Anthony, Robert. *Total Self-Confidence.* New York: Berkley Books, Second Edition 1979

Auden, W.H. and Kronenberger, Louis. The Faber Book Of Aphorisms. London: Faber and Faber Limited, 1964

Belkin, Lisa. *Life's Work: Confessions of an Unbalanced.* New York: Simon & Schuster, 2002

Branden, Nathaniel. *The Six Pillars of Self-Esteem.* New York: Bantam, 1994.

Bullock, Alan and Woodings, R.B. *The Fontana Dictionary Of Modern Thinkers.* London: Fontana Paperbacks, First Edition 1983

Chapman, Elwood N. *Attitude: Your Most Priceless Possession.* Menlo Park, Calif.: Crisp Publications Inc., 1987

Chopra, Deepak and Simon, David. *Grow Younger, Live Longer.* New York: Harmony Books, 2001

Clark, Henry C. *Compass of Society: Commerce And Absolutism In Old-Regime France.* Lanham, MD: Lexington Books, 2006

Comfort, Alex. *The New Joy of Sex.* New York: Pocket Books, 1972

Conroy, Pat. *Beach Music.* New York: Bantam Books, 1996

Cook, John. *The Book of Positive Quotations.* Minneapolis: Fairview Press, 2007

Cooper, Kenneth H. *Regaining the Power of Youth.* Nashville: Thomas Nelson Publishers, First Edition, 1998.

Covey, Stephen. *The Seven Habits of Highly Effective People.* New York: Free Press, 1989

Csikszentmihalyl, Mihaly. *Creativity.* New York: Harper Collins, First Edition, 1996

Daintith, John. *Quotations For Speeches*. London: Bloomsbury Publishing, Second Edition 1992

Dalal. A.S., *The Hidden Forces Of Life*. Sri Aurobindo Ashram Trust, India. First Edition 1990

DeAngelis, Barbara. *Real Moments for Lovers*. New York: Dell Publishing, 1995

Deiner, Ed. *Well-being: The Foundations of Hedonic Psychology*. New York: Russell Sage Foundation, 2003

Einstein, Albert. *Ideas and Opinions*. New York: Bonanza Books, First Edition, 1954

Einstein, Albert. *The Joys of Research*. Washington: Smithsonian Institution Press, 1981

Excerpta Medica Foundation. *Excerpta Medica* 1969

Fiatarone, M.A., E. C. Marks, N. D. Ryan, C. N. Meredith, L. A. Lipsitz and W. J. Evans, "High-intensity strength training in nonagenarians. Effects on skeletal muscle", *Journal of the American Medical Association*, Vol. 263 No. 22, June 13, 1990

Frank, Leonard Roy. Quotationary. Websters, NY: Random House, 1999

Friedman, Meyer, and Rosenman, Ray H. *Type A Behavior and Your Heart*. New York: Knopf, 1974.

Gardiner, W Lambert. *A History of Media*. Victoria, BC: Trafford Publishing, 2006

Gardner, John W. and Francesca. *Quotations Of Wit And Wisdom*. New York: WW Norton Company Inc., First Edition 1975

Gautami, Mamta, *IRONDOC: Practical Stress Management Tools for Physicians*. Ottawa: Book Coach Press, 2004

Gee, Renie. Who Said That? Cincinnati: F&W Publications, First Edition, 2004.

Gleason, Norma. *Proverbs from Around the World*. New York: Carol Publishing Group, First Edition 2002

Godek, Gregory. *1001 Ways to Be Romantic.* Weymouth, Mass.: Casablanca Press, 2000

Goleman, Daniel. *Emotional Intelligence: Why It Can Matter More than IQ.* New York: Bantam Books, 1995

Grothe, Mardy. *Oxymoronica.* New York; Harper-Collins, First Edition 2004

Grothe, Mardy. *Word Play for Word Lovers.* Harmondsworth, UK: Penguin Books, 1999

Greene, Graham. *The Heart of the Matter.* New York: Viking Press, 1948

Greene, Richard and Brize, Florie. *Words That Shook The World.* New York: Prentice Hall Press, First Edition 2002

Hardy, Thomas. *Under the Greenwood Tree.* Toronto: Penguin Classics, 1998

HarperCollins. *Quotation Finder.* Glasgow: HarperCollins, First Edition 1999

Heller, Joseph. *Something Happened.* New York: Random House, 1975

Henry, Lewis C. *Best Quotations for All Occasions.* Greenwich, Conn: Fawcett Publications, First Edition 1945

Hoffer, Eric. *The Passionate State of Mind.* New York: Harper, 1955

Holy Bible, New International Version. Colorado Springs: International Bible Society, 1973, 1978, 1984

Honoré, Carl. *In Praise of Slow: How a Worldwide Movement Is Challenging the Cult of Speed.* Toronto: Knopf Canada, 2004

Hyman, Mark and Liponis, Mark. *Ultra Prevention.* New York: Scribner, First Edition, 2003.

James, William. *The Principles of Psychology.* New York: Courier Dover Publications

Johnson, Philip. *Time Out.* Toronto: Stoddart Publishing, 1992

Jones, Charlie. *Quotes Are Tremendous.* Mechanicsburg, PA: Executive Books Publishers, 1995

Katz, Lawrence C. and Rubin, Manning. *Keep Your Brain Alive.* New York: Dell Publishing, First Edition, 1995.

Klein, Allen. *The Lift Your Spirits Quote Book.* New York: Random House, First Edition 2001

Klein, Allen. *The Wise And Witty Quote Book.* New York: Random House, Fourth Edition 2005

Kumove, Shirley. *Words Like Arrows.* Toronto: University Of Toronto Press, First Edition 1984

Kubistant, Tom. *Performing Your Best.* CITY, Life Enhancements Publications, 1986

Laozi, Philip J., *The Daodejing of Laoz.* Indianapolis: Hackett Publishing, 2003

Laurence, Tim. You Can Change Your Life. London: Hodder and Stoughton, First Edition, 2003.

Lebel, Gregory G. *Gro Harlem Brundtland, Development., Hal Kane, Our Common Future.* Oxford: Oxford University Press, 1987

Lindbergh, Anne Morrow. *Dearly Beloved: A Theme and Variations.* New York: Harcourt, Brace & World, 1962

Linfield, Jordan L. and Krevisk, Joseph. *Words of Love.* New York: Random House, Third Edition 2002

Loehr, Jim, and Schwartz, Tony. *The Power of Full Engagement: Managing Energy, Not Time, Is the Key to High Performance and Personal Renewal.* New York: Free Press, 2003

Luccock, Halford Edward. *Marching Off the Map: And Other Sermons.* New York: Harper, 1952

Masaldan, K.N. *A to Z Quotations.* New Delhi: New Light Publishers, First Edition

Maugham, William Somerset. *Collected Plays.* London: Heinemann, 1952

Mindell, Earl. *Diet Bible.* Gloucester, MA: Fair Winds Press, First Edition, 2002

Montagu, Ashley. *Growing Young*. New York: McGraw-Hill Book Company, 1981

Morgan, Arthur T. *Handbook Of Quotations*. Delhi: Goyl Saab Publishers, Second Edition 1993

Morley, Christopher. *Where Blue Begins*. Rockville, Md.: Wildside Press, 2001

O'Connor, Dagmar. *How to Make Love to the Same Person for the Rest of Your Life and Still Love It*. Garden City, N.Y.: Doubleday & Company, Inc., 1985

Osing, Richard A. How to Love and Be Loved. Arkansas City, KS: Rudi Publishing, Second Edition, 1999

Peale, Norman Vincent. *Enthusiasm Makes a Difference*: New York: Simon & Schuster, 1995

Peck, M. Scott. *Abounding Wisdom*. Kansas City: Andrews McMeel Publishing, 2002

Penn Arts and Sciences, Spring 1999
http://www.sas.upenn.edu/sasalum/newsltr/spring99/Shakespeare.html

Petras, Kathryn and Ross. *The Whole World Book Of Quotations*. Reading, Mass: Addison-Wesley Publishing, 1995

Pound, Richard W. *High Impact Quotations*. Markham, ON: Fitzhenry & Whiteside, First Edition 2004

Pressman, Alan H. and Buff, Sheila. *The Complete Idiot's Guide to Vitamins and Minerals*. Indianapolis: Alpha Books, Second Edition, 2000.

Price, Steven D. *1001 Smartest Things Ever Said*. Guilford, Conn.: The Lyons Press, 2004

Princeton Language Institute. *21st Century Dictionary Of Quotations*. New York: Random House, 1993

Rajanbabu, P. *A Handy Book Of Proverbs And Quotations*. Chennai: New Century Book House, Second Edition 1995

Reavley, Nicola. *New Encyclopaedia of Vitamins, Minerals, Supplements and Herbs*. New York: Bookman Press, First Edition, 1995

Robertson, Connie. *The Wordsworth Book Of Humorous Quotations.* Hertfordshire, UK: Wordsworth Editions Ltd., First Edition 1998

Roger, John, and McWilliams, Peter. *Comfort Zone.* Los Angeles: Prelude Press, 1991

Sachs, Jeffrey D. *The End of Poverty: Economic Possibilities of Our Time.* New York: Penguin Press, 2005

Saraswat, Mahendra. *Upkar's The World Of Inspiring Quotations.* Swadeshi Bima Nagar: Author & Publishers, First Edition

Shanahan, John M. *The Most Brilliant Thoughts Of All Time.* New York: Harper-Collins Publishers, First Edition 1999

Sharma, R.N., and Kumar, Mahendra. *Best Quotations.* Mandi, India: M. I. Publications, Second Edition

Singer, June. *William Blake, The Unholy Bible: A Psychological Interpretation of William Blake.* Published by Putnam for the C. G. Jung Foundation for Analytical Psychology, 1970

Smith, Dr. Timothy. *Renewal: The Anti-Aging Revolution.* New York: St. Martin's Paperbacks, 1998

Stevenson, Adlai Ewing. *Speeches.* New York: Random House, 1952

Taylor, Kenneth N. *The Living Bible.* Wheaton, Ill.: Tyndale House Publishers, Inc., 1971

Thayer, Robert E. *The Origin of Everyday Moods: Managing Energy, Tension, and Stress.* New York: Oxford University Press, USA, 1997

Tripp, Rhoda Thomas. *The International Thesaurus of Quotations.* New York: Crowell, 1970

Turkington, Carol A. *The Quotable Lover.* New York: McGraw Hill, First Edition 2000

Ursell, Amanda. *Vitamins and Minerals Handbook.* New York: Dorling Kindersley, First Edition, 2001

Van Mill, David. *Liberty, Rationality, and Agency in Hobbes's Leviathan.* Albany: SUNY Press, 2001

Winsten, Stephen. *The Quintessence of G.B.S.: The Wit and Wisdom of Bernard Shaw*. Hutchinson, 1949

Zend, Robert. *Beyond Labels*. Toronto: Hounslow Press, 1982

Information about much of the biographies referred to in this text was taken from:

www.wikipedia.org
www.online-literature.com
www.quotationspage.com
www.britannica.com
www.thefreelibrary.com
www.encarta.msn.com
www.google.com

Historical Bibliography

Adamic, Louis. *The Native's Return: An American Immigrant Visits Yugoslavia and Discovers...* New York: Harper & Brothers, 1934

Agnew, John Holmes Agnew and Littell, Eliakim. *The Eclectic Museum of Foreign Literature, Science and Art.* E. Littell, 1843

Aquinas, Thomas. *A Summa of the Summa: The Essential Philosophical Passages of St. Thomas.* Fort Collins, CO: Ignatius Press, 1990

Bacon, Francis Bacon. *The Essays Of Francis Bacon.* Boston: Houghton Mifflin, 1908

Ballou, Maturin Murray. *Notable Thoughts about Women: A Literary Mosaic.* Boston: Houghton Mifflin, 1882

Carlyle, Thomas. *The Works of Thomas Carlyle* (C. Scribner's Sons, 1899)

Chaucer, Geoffrey. *The Canterbury Tales: Being Selections from the Tales of Geoffrey Chaucer.* London: Chapman and Hall, 1884

Coleridge, Samuel Taylor. *Ancient Mariner.* Sampson Low, 1857

Coleridge. Samuel Taylor. *The Complete Works of Samuel Taylor Coleridge: With an Introductory Essay.* New York: Harper & Brothers, 1856

Cross, Joseph. *Portraiture and Pencilings of the Late Mrs. L.A.L. Cross.* Printed at the office of the *Nashville and Louisville Christian Advocate.* John Lellyett, printer, 1851

Dryden, John. *The Works of John Dryden.* Berkeley, CA: University of California Press, 1974

Eliot, T.S. *Selected Essays.* New York: Harcourt Brace, 1950

Emerson, Ralph Waldo. *The Works of Ralph Waldo Emerson.* G. Bell & Sons, 1906

Hazlitt, William. *William Ernest Henley, The Collected Works of William Hazlitt.* J.M. Dent & Co.; McClure, Phillips & Co, 1903

Johnson, Samuel. *The Works of Samuel Johnson.* Project Gutenberg, 1823

Jung, Carl Gustav, *Man and His Symbols*. Aldus Books in association with W. H. Allen, 1964

Kappa Delta Pi. *The Educational Forum*. Kappa Delta Pim, 1936

Keats, John. *The Finer Tone: Keats' Major Poems*. Baltimore: Johns Hopkins Press, 1953

Kierkegaard, Soren. *Kierkegaard,* Cassel, 1955

Laertius, Diogenes. *The Lives and Opinions of Eminent*. George Bell & Sons, 1895

Lowell, James Russell. *The Writings of James Russell Lowell*. Riverside Press, 1890

Masefield, John. *The Poems and Plays of John Masefield*. New York: The Macmillan Company, 1922

McWilliam, Andrew. *Percy Longmuir*. J.B. Lippincott Company, 1907

Middleton, Thomas. *The Works of Thomas Middleton*. J.C. Nimno, 1885

Mill, John Stuart. *On Liberty*. Ticknor and Fields, 1863

Pascal, Blaise. *Thoughts*. New York: Cosimo Inc. 2007

Scott, Walter. *The Poetical Works of Walter Scott*. Robert Cadell, 1820

Shakespeare. William. *William Shakespeare*. Hauppauge, NY: Barron's Educational Series, 2002

Shelley, Percy Bysshe. *The Complete Works of Percy Bysshe Shelley*. Virtue & Company, 1904

Stanley, Bessie. "What Constitutes Success," *Lincoln Sentinel*, 1905.

Thoreau, Henry David. *The Writings of Henry David Thoreau*. Boston: Houghton Mifflin, 1937

Thoreau, Henry David. *Journal*, Aug. 21, 1851

Whitman, Walt. *Walt Whitman*. New York: Sterling Publishing Company, Inc., 1997

Wordsworth, William. *The Poetical Works of William Wordsworth*. Phillips, Sampson and Company, 1856

Image Credits

Yoga images courtesy of Michelle Landry, Digital Dragon Designery, Victoria B.C.

The Scream is courtesy of www.angelo.edu .

Photographs of Saturn, sunflowers, the Pyramids and the Taj Mahal, courtesy of www.istockphoto.com

The author is available to give a
lecture/seminar/workshop
on

Practical Wisdom
for a Finer Life

Please contact:

Professor James Nicholas

www.wisdomanddelight.com
wisdomanddelight@hotmail.com
613-741-7576
1403-158B McArthur Ave
Ottawa, Ontario, Canada
K1L 8C9

Copies of *A Book of Wisdom and Delight* can
be purchased online at www.iuniverse.com/
bookstore